Wetheral and Great Corby

an illustrated history

Denis Perriam & David Ramshaw

P3 Publications

2008

www.p3publications.com

Foreword & Acknowledgements

Foreword

It is over fifty years since Margaret Kirkpatrick wrote *The Story of Wetheral* and forty years since this was last reprinted. As nothing has appeared since, a new work on this subject is long overdue. The two villages of Wetheral and Great Corby lie side by side separated only by the Eden and one cannot be mentioned without the other. For this reason both have been combined in one volume. An illustrated history was thought by the authors the best means of telling the story of the villages. In 2008 an exhibition on Wetheral and Great Corby was launched, with images and material derived from Keith Simmond's vast collection on the two villages. Keith's enthusiasm for the area, his invaluable photographs and his willingness to share his collection with others were major factors in making this book a viable proposition. There are gaps in the history of these two villages and this is in part deliberate, making it possible for the present authors or someone else to produce a future volume. The hope is that, as a result of reading this book, individuals will come forward with additional material to justify a second edition!

Acknowledgements

The authors would like to acknowledge the help given by many people and organisations in the preparation of this book. In particular we thank Melanie Gardner of Tullie House Museum and Art Gallery for making available images of paintings in the city's collection, Stephen White of Carlisle Library and David Bowcock of Cumbria Record Office for information and images and Dr John Storr and Keith Simmonds for making their libraries of photographs available to us. Newspaper cuttings and illustrations have been reproduced with the permission of Cumbrian Newspapers. Many thanks also to Frances Apps, Charles Armstrong, Joe Armstrong, Dorothy Carruthers, Bettie Baird, John Delap, Hazel Downie, Bill Fawcett, Mary Ferguson, Michael Finlay, Anna Gray, David Grisenthwaite, Nigel Holmes, Patrick Horton, John Huggon, Eric Judge, Ashley Kendall, Dorothy Smithson, Vera Timperon and David Weston for historical information as well as photographs relating to past residents, businesses and other matters.

Thank you also to the many individuals, too many to mention here by name, who contributed the occasional snippet of information or image. Every effort has been made to contact copyright holders for permission to use photographs and throughout the book these are credited with the provider's name. Unattributed modern photographs were taken by David Ramshaw.

Contents

The Origins of Corby and Wetheral

With the River Eden as a means of transportation it is possible that stone quarried at Wetheral was used in the construction of Hadrian's Wall. Quarry face inscriptions at Gelt Woods and Wetheral show the presence of the 20th Legion, different cohorts of that regiment doing much of the work on the wall.

The place names of Wetheral and Great Corby suggest early settlement. Corby is thought to be Irish-Scandinavian, 'kork'; meaning 'oats'.

Wetheral has a number of possibilities. Margaret Kirkpatrick has suggested that the name 'Wetheral' could be derived from the Anglo-Saxon 'weder' for sheep and 'healh' for a steep, grassy slope. However, *Place Names of Cumberland* thinks this could be 'Wether' and 'Haugh' meaning 'low pasture'.

There was an ancient ford which explains later settlement here, the villages having developed to serve both the priory at Wetheral and the castle at Corby. The road layout in each village is medieval.

Keith Simmonds

Above: Photograph of one of the Wetheral Woods Roman inscriptions taken about 1980 when still in situ. The inscription reads "MAXIMUS SCRIPSIT" which translates "Maximus wrote this".

Above: The rock fragment photographed at Tullie House Museum in 2008.

National Trust/Robert Maxwell

Left: The Roman inscription on the riverbank near Wetheral Cells (see page 7) has been known for many years. Unfortunately in 1991, due to erosion, the rock carrying the inscription came loose and fell down the riverbank, so the National Trust removed it for safe keeping. The team entrusted with that task are seen here retrieving it. The stone was initially stored at Loweswater before being given to Tullie House Museum in March 2005, where it is now in store.

Right: A photograph taken in 2008 of the other inscription still in situ in Wetheral Woods. This inscription reads: "LEG XX. V V CONDRAUSISIUS" followed by an image of a stag. Translated this reads: "Condrausisius of the Twentieth Legion Valerie Victrix."

Wetheral Cross

Left: The estimated height of the cross in relation to a human figure.

Left: The base of the 1751 sundial in the churchyard is probably the re-used socket stone which supported the cross.

The Dean and Chapter, Carlisle Cathedral

Above: The one surviving arm of the cross has been used to clone the others for this reconstruction.

The eminent architectural historian, Howard Colvin (later knighted), was on a visit to Wetheral about 1965 when he noticed amongst the rubble of the monuments cleared from the churchyard the sculptured arm of an early cross. Anglo-Saxon lettering was inscribed on the reverse of the stone. He realised the importance of the find, but for some reason took it back to Oxford and did not make the find generally known. It appeared for the first time in Bailey and Cramp's, *Corpus of Anglo-Saxon Stone Sculpture,* in 1988.

Professor Rosemary Cramp dates the stone to the 8th or 9th century, stating, "this was obviously part of an impressive Anglican Monument." Although only a fragment of lettering survived, Professor Cramp said, "inscriptions point to a literate community associated with the site and it is possible that this derived from a monastic site." From this one piece it is possible to reconstruct what the cross-head may have looked like, seen here for the first time. This would have been visible at a considerable height on an elaborately decorated shaft and associated with a religious site which pre-dated the present church and priory. The significance of this find to the early history of Wetheral has not been fully appreciated. In 2007 the stone was returned to the area, and a decision on its future location has yet to be determined.

Wetheral Priory

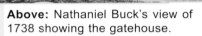

The earliest records for the two villages are after the Norman conquest. Ranulf Meschin was the first Norman Lord of Cumberland and, about 1112, founded Wetheral Priory for 12 Benedictine monks. The estate, which included all the lands of the manor of Wetheral, was given to Stephen, the abbot of St Mary's, York. Ranulf granted the monks the important concession of having a sluice and fish pond on the River Eden and a mill, which was not to be "interfered with" by the Lord of Corby. As with other northern priories there was a right of sanctuary conferred by Henry 1, when he endowed Wetheral Priory with all the customs and liberties enjoyed by the churches of St Peter in York and St John in Beverley.

Ralf Hartley, the last prior was probably installed to facilitate the Act of Dissolution because the document of surrender did not carry the seal of the house, only the prior's seal. Ralf was awarded a pension of £20 later revised to £12 plus the rectory of Wetheral and Warwick. On 31 December 1538 the commissioners of surrender, Sir Thomas Wharton and James Rokebie, sold various church utensils including alabaster tables, brass candlesticks, choir stalls etc. One of the bells from the priory went to Carlisle to be hung on Springall Tower and used to, "call the workmen to worke at the making of the new cytydall in Carlyle and mending of the castell there."

The buildings soon fell into decay and were not repaired. Thomas Denton, writing in 1687, stated that only the gatehouse remained entire and in good repair. It probably survived because it was used as a vicarage for the minister. It would also be a good refuge from night raiders with the chambers above the arch only accessible via a narrow stone spiral staircase.

Above: Nathaniel Buck's view of 1738 showing the gatehouse.

Above: Inside the gatehouse the floors are missing today, but it is in a sound state and cared for by English Heritage, who open it to the public. A spiral staircase leads one up to the rooms above the gatehouse.

Left: Thomas Hearne visited in 1778 and made a watercolour drawing of the gatehouse. This is a copy of the original painting by Mary Slee, an art teacher and miniaturist from Carlisle.

Wetheral Cells

The fireplace in the front wall.

'St Constantine's Cells' by Luke Clennell, 1814, showing the position above the river.

The cells are three ancient vaulted rooms carved out of the solid cliff face on the west bank of the Eden, south of the Wetheral Priory site. They were variously known as Wetheral Safeguards, St Constantine's Cells and Constantine's Hermitage.

If you walk the path from the old Wetheral ferry landing, that leads upstream into Wetheral Woods (now a National Trust property), and keep to the lower path when the path splits, you soon arrive at stone steps leading down to the entrance of the Wetheral Cells. In the past they were probably better concealed and they may have been used for emergency food storage for the priory, or the storage of their valuables in troubled times. However, there is a fireplace in the front wall overlooking the river, which suggests that they may also have been used as a refuge for the monks against Border raiders who made many forays into Cumberland in the 13th and 14th centuries, stealing cattle and other goods and killing anyone that opposed them.

Carvings near the cells

Captain William Mounsey of Castle Street, Carlisle, spent his leisure time carving quotations on rock faces near the Eden. Two of these are close to the Wetheral Cells and the first one can be seen in the rock face halfway down the steps. The main text (below) is a verse from the songs of Llywarch Hen, a Welsh poet of the early 9th century. It translates: "This leaf which is being persecuted by the wind, let her beware of her fate: She is old though only born this year".

Left: Entrance to the cells.

A second inscription, about 20 metres downstream from the first, reads:
To meet the Atlantic's boundless time,
See old Ituna's waters glide,
As rolls the river to the sea
So time unto eternity.
O mVo AD 1852

YESNUOM SUMLEILVG
The signature at the bottom is Gulielmus (William) Mounsey written backwards and *Ituna* is the Roman name for the River Eden

Wetheral Church

Ashley Kendall.

Photographs taken at the beginning of the 20th century show the crowded graveyard. Gravestones were often whitewashed regularly by the surviving family with the lettering picked out in black.

Nigel Holmes.

Past histories of Wetheral have concentrated on the church and it is unnecessary for such repetition here. Readers who want further information on this should refer to the bibliography.

Parts of the medieval structure survive, to which has been added the Howard Chapel. The present appearance of the church dates from 1881 when the earlier square tower was replaced with the octagonal one of today.

This church originally served a much wider parish and, of the gravestones that survive, few are actually from the village of Wetheral. Fortunately, before the stones were removed, a survey was made to record the inscriptions and position of each one.

Ashley Kendall

Denis Perriam

Maria, the wife of Henry Howard, died in childbirth at Corby Castle in 1788, aged 22 (her 23rd year).

Her distraught husband had a special chapel erected at the church (seen above with distinctive pinnacles) to house a marble monument (left) by one of the leading sculptors of the day, Joseph Nollekens. This was one of Nollekens' major works and cost £1500. When Nollekens heard that his statue was to be placed in Wetheral Church, he apparently burst into tears, upset that one of his finest pieces was going somewhere where it would not be seen by admirers of his work.

However, his tomb in Paddington Church (upper left) shows the sculptor re-united with his famous work at Wetheral.

Wetheral Church

Keith Simmonds both images

Above: An early photograph (circa 1870) of Wetheral Church with the original square tower.

Above: The Parochial Council outside the old vicarage.

Churchyard inspections by the local sanitary authority in the 1880s proved that Wetheral was overcrowded and at capacity. After a new burial ground was opened for internments, the original graveyard was left to slowly deteriorate until it became unsightly and dangerous. In 1964 a decision was made to clear the graveyard, but it was much later that this was achieved, leaving a small number of headstones in situ.

Cumberland News 29 May 1964

CHURCHYARD WORK DELAYS CRITICISED

DELAY in renovations to Wetheral closed Church-yard was criticised at Wednesday's annual meeting of the Parish Council in the Village Hall at Wetheral.

Mr A. Pattinson said renovations and improvements in the Churchyard were delayed in discussion. It was two or three years since they had decided to have the Churchyard renovated.

The new chairman of the Council, who was elected at Wednesday's meeting, Mrs D. C. Carruthers, said: "The work is going ahead, I believe, but it takes some time to make records, etc. I think we had better leave it to the fullness of time.

Below: An 1840s lithograph of the church by George Hildebrande. Just to the right of the tower is the vicarage which overlooked the Green (demolished in 1952).

Keith Simmonds

Wetheral Cemetery

Canon Loftie, writing in 1923 in his book on Wetheral, said "the extensive churchyard lying round the church on every side, and extending down almost to the river bank is plainly seen from its numerous monuments and gravestones to be quite occupied by burials ... there does not seem to be a spot left unused ... so we do not wonder that about 1890 it was closed for burials by an order in council." The Dean and Chapter offered a field down by the river bank, which Canon Loftie thought, "would have been much more suitable than the land afterwards purchased as a cemetery, but it was not accepted for some reason by the committee." The site eventually chosen was regarded by Loftie, "a very inconvenient distance for the funerals of those who desired to have the service in the church before the burial in the cemetery."

This delay in laying out and consecrating the land caused some inconvenience. It took even longer to erect a cemetery chapel and for the two acre site to be "planted with trees and shrubs and ornamented with flower borders." The consecration was performed, in 1892, by Dr Ware, the Bishop of Barrow-in-Furness, and with that part being full, a further consecration for an extension was carried out by the Bishop of Carlisle in 1921. This is still in use today, but for those who wish, ashes are buried in the former churchyard, marked by a communial stone near the church.

The Ling family stone, designed by J H Martindale in 1904.

Above: In 1913 the horse-drawn funeral cortege for Christopher Ling makes its way from Wetheral Church to the cemetery. The Reverends Scott and Loftie lead with curate MacFarlane behind. The photo illustrates the arduous uphill struggle from the church to the cemetery.

Left: The chapel in the cemetery.

Chapels

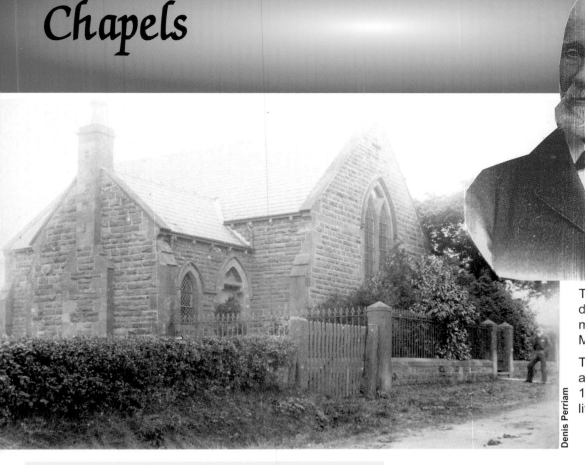

Cumbria Record Office

Thomas Burrow, described as "the first man" of Wetheral Methodist chapel.

The Wesleyan chapel at Wetheral in the 1890s, which remains little changed today.

Denis Perriam

From 1868 Methodist services were held in the house of Thomas Burrow. In 1871 a piece of land was offered for the building of a Wesleyan chapel with the first stone laid on 15 April 1873. The building cost of £440 was covered by the congregation. The Wetheral chapel remains in use today, although Wesleyan has been dropped from the title.

In 1889 a Methodist chapel was built at Great Corby, which was in use for almost a century, but, with a dwindling congregation, this closed on 18 June 1986.

Below: Chapel poster of 1875 and an early Sunday School group at Wetheral chapel.

John Huggon (both images)

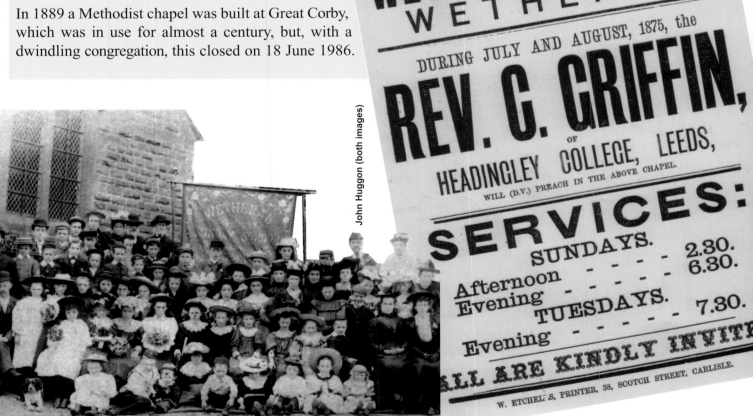

WESLEYAN CHAPEL, WETHERAL.

DURING JULY AND AUGUST, 1875, the

REV. C. GRIFFIN,

OF

HEADINGLEY COLLEGE, LEEDS,

WILL (D.V.) PREACH IN THE ABOVE CHAPEL.

SERVICES:

SUNDAYS.
Afternoon - - - - 2.30.
Evening - - - - 6.30.

TUESDAYS.
Evening - - - - 7.30.

ALL ARE KINDLY INVITE

W. ETCHELLS, PRINTER, 33, SCOTCH STREET, CARLISLE.

Corby Castle

Above: The Howard Coat of Arms.

Left: Corby Castle in 1906.

Michael Finlay

Norman baronies were divided into manors and Corby manor was part of the barony of Gilsland. Corby was further divided into two, Little and Great Corby, under one lord who had his seat at Great Corby, where the castle is today. There was an early manor house which was mentioned in the 12th & 13th centuries as having a chapel. After Bannockburn in 1314, no landowning family was safe from Scottish incursion and it was necessary to build a strong tower for security. This was a good defensive site and, over the years additional buildings were added to the tower, so that eventually, under the Howards, the castle became the imposing mansion it is today. Much of what can be seen today dates from the early 19th century, with the main facades surmounted by stone lions - the family crest of the Howards.

Corby Castle Caves in the sandstone cliff below the castle.

Liz Hodgson

Corby Castle from Wetheral Woods in 2008.

Manorial Rights

Carlisle Library

Left: Thomas Allom's view of the coops in 1832, looking similar to those of today, with a view of Corby Castle in the distance.

Below Centre: The fish coops in 2008, seen from the Wetheral side of the river.

Below: A fisherman and his gillie posing for the camera with a salmon catch.

Reg Elliot

Reg Elliot

Above: John Elliot, father of Reg Elliot (see page 68), who was a gillie at the castle. Here in the 1930s he displays a good catch of salmon. The upstream grills or "lechs" as they are called are clearly seen in the foreground.

The salmon coops on the Eden at Corby are purported to be one of the oldest functioning river fish traps in the UK. A fishery on the Corby side of the river was granted to Wetheral Priory in the 12th century. After the Dissolution of the Monasteries the fishing rights were transferred to Carlisle Cathedral and leased back by the Howards of Corby.

Although of no great antiquity and needing constant refurbishment, the coops are Grade 1 listed because they are unique in the country. Sluice gates and boxes were designed to catch salmon as they swam upstream to spawn. Once common, salmon are now a rarity on the Eden.

Corby Walks

Left: John Robinson, an amateur artist and son of the publican of the Queen Inn, Great Corby, painted this view of Corby Walks, probably in the 1860s.

Below: Polyphemus, or the 'Corby Giant', graced the walk to the river from the Castle. His size can be judged by comparison with these individuals about 1900.

In 1831, Mrs Catherine Howard wrote that the garden walks were "graced by a number of sphinxes, sea-horses, gods and goddesses." However she went on to condemn, "the destructive propensity so innate in the English, that, when the pleasure grounds are opened to everyone, they left neither a seat nor the smooth bark of a tree unmutilated with names and low verses; not even a statue or Roman altar escaped from being broken to atoms and thrown into the river." Extreme caution was exercised when advertising in the *Journal* on 29 July 1815, that the gardens were open. "Corby walks are to be shown on Wednesdays only ... no person will be admitted without asking for the gardener, who will be ready to attend the company round the pleasure grounds." Access was restricted. "Not more than 12 persons will be allowed to see the walks at a time and they are requested not to bring dogs." Only the gentry were welcome as the notice continued, "Carriages are to remain at the inn at Corby Village."

No reason was given in the paper at the time to explain why these restrictions had been imposed, but in the *Journal,* 1 January 1825, was the following, "Polyphemus, the gigantic statue so well known to visitors at Corby Castle, has lately been re-headed and will soon, to use a popular phrase, be 'himself again'." The circumstances behind this were given. "About 20 years ago [1805] a party of miscreants procured admission to these beautiful and romantic walks; one of whom, having espied the brazen eye in the forehead of Polyphemus, proceeded to scramble up the adjoining rock and forced off the head of the Cyclops and after picking out the eye, threw the fragment of the head into the River Eden." The golden eye had been made of semi-precious stone and fixed in a recess of the forehead of the statue which was over 12ft high. In a guide book of 1847 Isaac Fletcher Whitridge stated that, "when the head was put back, another eye of a less valuable material was put in its place."

Sir John Clerk visited on 5 September 1734 recording in his journal, "in the afternoon we went and viewed Corby Castle, the seat of Mr Howard. This place is by nature exceedingly charming and indeed so full of natural beuties [sic] that I think no place of my acquaintance in Britain is equal to it."

The Howards chose not to live at Corby Castle and it was let, but the tradition of opening to the public was continued. Mr Behrens, who had taken a ten year lease, admitted visitors to the grounds on Wednesdays from 10.30am to 6pm, but, "each name was to be recorded in a book at the entrance gate and no large parties without prior booking."

The last tenant, Judge Hills, left to take Highhead Castle in 1902, and Philip Howard returned to occupy the family seat. With ever-increasing numbers of visitors to the castle grounds in the 1920s, there was further vandalism. When a Greek inscription on one of the statues on the walk was scratched out in the summer of 1925, Mr Howard sent a strongly worded letter to the editor of the *Journal*, "In consequence of this the grounds will very shortly have to be closed to the public." Philip Howard made clear the extent of the problem. " I may add that not so long ago four small tombstones, each lettered, the memorials of as many faithful and loyal companions, dogs of choice and rare breeds, were ruthlessly thrown down and broken in a part of the grounds." The editorial in the same paper pointed out that, "many beautiful places to which public admission was once freely given have been closed against strangers on account of the damage and annoyance which were caused by people who were incapable of appreciating the privilege which they abused and now the lovely Corby Grounds are to be placed in the same category."

The editorial ended: "The pity is that the majority should have to suffer for the fault of a few selfish and ignorant hooligans." Fortunately the grounds were re-opened to the public again.

Carlisle Library

Above: Seen to its best from Wetheral this view by Nathaniel Buck in 1738 shows the cascade as it appeared shortly after construction.

Sir John Clerk continued: "At the end of the walk next the house is a cascade 140 feet high....not quite finished but is, however, the finest I believe in England.
The statues are all of stone but not very well done...one of these representing Polephemus [sic], which serves for a vista to this fine walk.
Mr Howard himself met us ...and he showed me a passage in Milton's Paradise where he describes the Garden of Eden which very nearly resembles the description one would give of Corby Castle."

John Storr

Joe Armstrong

Above: At the turn of the 20th century the cascade had become overgrown but it took another century before it was brought back to its former glory (see left).

Lords of the Manor

Tullie House Museum & Art Gallery

The Tullie family coat-of-arms.

Tullie House in 1891, watercolour by Thomas Bushby.

From the late17th century the Tullie family held the lease of Wetheral Manor from the Dean & Chapter entitling them to be lords of the manor. The Tullies then sub-let the farm, Cotehouse and the mill (see page 20). In 1728 John Waugh, son of a bishop of Carlisle, married Isabella Tullie, a daughter of Thomas Tullie, for whom Tullie House in Abbey Street had been built. Dr Waugh was rector of Caldbeck, vicar of Stanwix and a canon of Carlisle Cathedral. In 1730 he was appointed Chancellor of the Diocese of Carlisle and moved with his family into Eaglesfield House in Abbey Street, directly opposite Tullie House. He died in 1765 and was buried in Carlisle Cathedral. His wife, Isabella, had two elder brothers, Jerome Tullie and William Tullie. Jerome lived in Tullie House until his death in 1756 but William, a lawyer in London, chose not to live in the family house when he succeeded his brother. Isabella and family then moved across the road into Tullie House, which she later inherited, with her sister, Anne Cornthwaite, as co-heir.

When Isabella died in 1775 she left five unmarried daughters in Tullie House, where they lived in great style "in the greatest harmony." Few people in 18th century Carlisle could afford a coach pulled by four horses, but this was kept by the Misses Waugh. In Dorothy Wordsworth's *Tour of Scotland* she refers to, "the renowned Miss Waughs travelling in state in a coach and four with servants on horseback ... the old ladies as gaily dressed as bullfinches in spring." They are also remembered for an indoor male servant, one of many, who wore blue and yellow livery. The Waugh sisters were particularly fond of Wetheral and often visited the village. As granddaughters of a former bishop they had been allowed to occupy prebendal seats in the Cathedral until, in 1781, they were ousted by the Dean. This so offended them that they never set foot in the Cathedral again and attended Wetheral Church from then on.

The funeral of Mary Waugh was equal to the lifestyle that she and her sisters had enjoyed. Her nephew, Tullie Joseph Cornthwaite, who inherited Tullie House, was there to witness the event, "We buried Mrs Waugh on Monday last in full parade in this county." All ladies of eminence were then given the title of

Sacred to the Memory

OF

THE FIVE SISTERS WAUGH,
DAUGHTERS OF DR. JOHN WAUGH,
LATE DEAN OF WORCESTER,
AND ISABELLA TULLIE, HIS WIFE;
WHO LIVED TOGETHER IN THE GREATEST HARMONY,
AND DIED UNIVERSALLY ESTEEMED AND REGRETTED.
TO THE CHURCH THEY WERE MOST ZEALOUSLY ATTACHED,
AND TO THE POOR
UNCEASINGLY CHARITABLE.
FEW PERSONS WERE BETTER KNOWN,
AND FEW MORE RESPECTED.

JUDITH WAUGH, DIED 29 JULY, 1799, AGED 67.
MARGARET WAUGH, DIED 31 JANUARY, 1803, AGED 59.
ISABELLA WAUGH, DIED 28 NOVEMBER, 1809, AGED 72.
ELIZABETH WAUGH, DIED 26 FEBRUARY, 1814, AGED 70.
MARY WAUGH, DIED 9 APRIL, 1815, AGED 75.

Right: Mr Cornthwaite's niece, Eliza Rivaz and a nephew, the Rev. Baden Powell, married.
Lord Baden Powell, founder of the Scout Movement, was thus related to the Tullie family.
One of the Baden Powells wrote to the vicar of Wetheral in 1931 to ask about this relationship.
Left: A wall plaque in Wetheral Church records the Waughs.

Mrs even if they were Miss. He went on to describe the funeral as it left Tullie House in April 1815, "a hearse and four and her own carriage with two servants behind." These were followed by, "eight gentlemen's carriages with various friends and acquaintants being complemented with scarves, gloves, hat bands, rings etc."

"We made a grand parade and bustle," he said and estimated, "no fewer than 2000 people were collected round the house and followed the hearse for three or four miles on the road to Wetheral." They arrived at Wetheral at 2pm and returned to Tullie House at 4pm, where Mr Cornthwaite stated there was, "plenty of eating and drinking similar to a wedding with us, or an heir coming of age." He thought, "the expenses of the funeral will be short of £500 - Miss Betty's [Elizabeth Waugh's in 1814] cost near £400 and fell far short of this."

Mr Cornthwaite, as executor of the last Miss Waugh's will, had to stay on in Carlisle to clear Tullie House, which he related in a letter to his brother-in-law, "I have been busily employed in looking over and burning old letters but have found no papers of any consequence but the will - no directions of any sort about servants, mourning rings or anything else which makes it very unpleasant as I have to guess at every thing without the least insight into her affairs." The Wetheral estate he thought to be worth about £1000 per annum. Tullie House was then put up for sale and it was purchased by Colonel Richard Salkeld in 1817. Some of the furniture was packed off to London where the Cornthwaites lived. Other items were given to Henry Howard of Corby Castle as a keepsake of his friendship with the Waughs and the remainder was left in the house for the Colonel.

Three of the Waugh sisters, pastels by an unknown artist.

Wetheral Folly

On the river bank to the south of Wetheral stood a rather unusual building with three turrets which few people remember, although it stood until 1962. This was Wetheral Folly. Had there been a suitable house at Wetheral the Misses Waugh may have taken it, but instead they decided to build one. On 23 June 1792 the Dean and Chapter gave permission for them, "to cut wood at Wetheral for a summer house." The Folly was constructed on land belonging to Abbey Farm and seems to be the place where the sisters spent their summers. The appearance of the house was as eccentric as they were. However they did not live long enough to enjoy their retreat.

William Hutchinson illustrated the Folly in his *History of Cumberland* in 1794, shortly after it had been completed for the Waugh family.

In Thurnam's *Guide to Carlisle* of 1821 it was stated, " a little higher up the river stands a large summerhouse, erected in the Gothic Style, by the late Miss Waughs of Carlisle. The building is on a peculiarly fine situation, and it is to be regretted that one so utterly devoid of beauty, and so ill according with the scene around, should have been placed where one of a different kind would have had so fine an effect."

Few further details of Wetheral Folly are given, but it seems to have remained with the Cornthwaite family until the lease on Abbey Farm was allowed to lapse in the mid-19th century. The Folly was then let by the Dean and Chapter. Archdeacon Prescott rented the Folly in November 1890 for an annual payment of £5. When Mr Milburn rented it in October 1920 the rental had increased to £10.

QUINQUE WAUGH SACREM HABUERE SORORES ET HILARITATI AMIGITÆ

Proposed alterations by JH Martindale in the 1920s did not include piped water or electricity although a metered water supply was put in in 1932. This did not deter people from living there and successive families made it their home until just after the war. Photographs in the *Journal,* 3 June 1955, showed how the unoccupied Folly had been damaged by vandals and it did not survive for long, being demolished for safety reasons. Luckily the arch from the Folly door was preserved and is now incorporated into the kitchen chimney piece of Acorn Bank, Wetheral. The date stone is also at Acorn Bank.

Had the Folly stood today it would have been a much sought after residence with a magnificent view over the wooded river banks below.

Left: Over a door on the Folly was a Latin inscription, recording that the Waughs had built it. This was saved on demolition along with the datestone (centre) of 1794.

Folly

Above: The interior of the Folly in Archdeacon Prescott's time, sparsely furnished and with fishing tackle on the table.

Above right: Archdeacon John Eustace Prescott about to go fishing in the Eden with the Folly in the background.

A keen fisherman, the Venerable John Eustace Prescott was often to be seen at the Folly during his thirty-year tenancy. He was the son of George Prescott, a merchant from Gibraltar and had come to Carlisle as the vicar of St Mary's in 1877. From 1883 he was Canon residentiary at the Cathedral and Archdeacon of Carlisle, becoming Chancellor of the Diocese in 1900. His interest in Wetheral is evident from the *Register of Wetheral Priory* which he wrote in 1897.

Iona Lady Molesworth-St Aubyn (all images on this page)

Above: Another Prescott family photograph of the Folly, probably taken in the 1890s.

Left: A visit to the Folly was often a family affair. This photograph of the Folly in mist featuring Archdeacon and Mrs Prescott (Rosalie Alcock) with daughter-in-law Lucy Prescott and her child Evelyn Rosalie, mother of Iona Lady Molesworth-St Aubyn.

Wetheral Mill

Wetheral Mill as it appears today with various modifications.

In the past the right to mill was in the hands of the lord of the manor and in the case of Wetheral this was the Priory. Usually there was only one corn mill per manor and those within the manor were to take their corn there to be made into flour, from which a portion was taken by the miller on behalf of the lord. Mills were served by a millrace and would always be on the same site from earliest times, although the mill buildings and wheel would need occasional replacement.

The mill which is there today looks 19th century as does the walling for the millrace and all that is missing is the mill-wheel. Documentary evidence show the existence of the mill, millpool and weir, from the 12th century, but it ceased to be the property of the Priory on Dissolution in 1540. In 1588 it was valued at 66s 8d (£3.33p in today's money). From then on the mill was in the hands of sub-tenants under the lord of the manor and the list of millers changed frequently, a lease sometimes lasting for only seven years. A complete list of millers would be difficult to compile, but in the 19th century there was Isaac Dodd in 1834 and Nathan Rowantrees in 1858, to name two.

In reminiscences in the *Journal* in 1894, one old inhabitant said, "It was quite common for people who took their batches to the mill to get ground, to wait till it was done and take it home with them." He added that it was usually barley, "for barley bread was chiefly used, especially among the working classes." Instead of cash changing hands, the correspondent said, "the miller paid himself out of the grain, taking out a certain proportion of the quantity ground."

The last miller, William Willis, may have started grinding grain, but was at the end, turning gypsum (probably from Cocklakes) into plaster of Paris. He advertised for qualified workmen for this purpose in 1876. It seems the mill retained its wheel because it was used to pump water from the river to the village. This stopped when it was realised that sewage was causing contamination and an alternative source was found. When Willis left the mill the tenancy was advertised in the *Journal* (10 January 1879);

Carlisle Library

The mill in 1836 showing the millrace flowing through the buildings and sacks of flour being taken out to a waiting cart. Lithograph by Matthew Nutter.

WATER CORN MILL and PREMISES at WETHERAL. To be Let and entered upon immediately, all that convenient and newly Erected Water Corn Mill, with good Dwelling House, Out-buildings, Stable, Piggeries, &c., adjoining, situate at Wetheral, about Four Miles from Carlisle, on the North-Eastern Railway.—Apply to Messrs. Saul, Solicitors, Castle Street, Carlisle.

Next at the mill was the Diocesan surveyor, Alexander Ormiston. For sometime the Ormistons remained at the mill, into the 20th century, and it stands as a number of houses today, suitably divided.

Wetheral Abbey Farm

Carlisle Journal

TO BUILDERS.

TENDERS WANTED for the BUILDING and FINISHING of a NEW HOUSE and FARM BUILDINGS, at WETHERAL ABBEY, near Carlisle.
Plans and Specifications may be examined, and every other information obtained at the Office of Mr. JAMES STEWART, Architect, Carlisle, where Tenders for the whole or for the several departments of work are to be delivered on or before the 6th day of MAY next.
The lowest or any Tender will not necessarily be accepted.
Carlisle, 23rd April, 1857.

Above: The advert in the *Journal* in 1857 asking for tenders to build the Abbey farmhouse and buildings.

Left: Abbey farmhouse today.

Wetheral Abbey Farm lies directly on top of the former priory and dates from the Dissolution when the ruined buildings and surrounding land were let by the Dean & Chapter for agricultural use. The farm was part of the manor and was let, together with the mill and fishery, and then sub-let. From the late 17th century the Tullie family, as lords under the Dean & Chapter, let to the Nicholsons and by the 19th century the Grahams were tenants. As this was a large farm the sitting tenant had status in the village being regarded as minor gentry, almost on a par with the Tullie family. Much of the priory was cleared by the 19th century and new buildings were planned in 1857. One of the workmen on this project was taken to court for bad time keeping, a breach of his contract. They were supposed to start at dawn on Monday mornings (perhaps staying all week), but as the workman explained he had to walk from Carlisle and it was, "very unreasonable to expect a man to be at work five miles away at 6am."

The importance of the ruin was being appreciated by the end of the century and on 15 June 1897 the Dean & Chapter made provision for the priory wall (not the gatehouse), "to be carefully repaired." It was recorded in the Dean & Chapter order book on 19 August 1924 that the Abbey Gatehouse had been scheduled by HM Office of Works as an Ancient Monument and as such ceased to be part of the farm, although this had in the past been the main entrance into the farmyard.

Above: Parts of the original priory walls can still be found in the farmyard, probably those repaired in 1897.

Below: Detail from the 1840s lithograph of Wetheral Church (see page 7) showing the farmhouse, gatehouse, gin gan (or horse thresher; the three sided building attached to the barn) and the Fish Inn (foreground).

Keith Simmonds

Inglewood Forest

All of the west bank of the Eden was within the Forest of Inglewood, one of the largest royal forests in England. This included all villages and even Carlisle and Penrith. Not all was wooded but was subject to Forest Law to control hunting, which was reserved for the king. There were concessions to allow peasants rights, to collect dead wood and graze certain animals. Little remained in royal ownership by the 19th century and with enclosure, any waste or common land was sold. Rights of warren were claimed by the Dean and Chapter with an annual hunt.

Wetheral Woods came within the forest but this was claimed as part of the manor of Wetheral. Visitors were allowed free access to the woods and in July 1881 the *Journal* said of the "lucrative passenger traffic to Wetheral during the summer ... the chief resort of the pleasure seekers was Wetheral Woods." As can be seen in these views firewood was regularly gathered in the woods. The boy in the painting (on the

Tullie House Museum & Art Gallery

Firewood Gatherers, Wetheral Woods, by Thomas Bushb (both images)

Ashley Kendall

Firewood Gatherers, Wetheral Woods.   Thos. Bushby

right), Billy Watt, recalled years later that Mr Bushby had said, "Come here I want to sketch you." Billy ran off and it was later that the artist caught up with him. Mistakenly Billy had thought Mr Bushby had said he wanted to 'skelp' him (beat him).

In 1895 the *Journal* gave recollections of Wetheral by "the oldest inhabitant." He said:

"as coals were so dear and some had great difficulty in getting them, sticks were very eagerly sought after, and the farmers had some trouble in keeping their hedges in repair, for no sooner were hedge stakes and yedders put in than they were pulled out and taken away to burn and none would admit taking them. One farmer hit upon a scheme to discover the pilferers. He bored a hole in a few of the stakes, put in a small quantity of gunpowder, and pegged up the holes. As usual the stakes soon began to be missing and an old woman that had taken them put one on the fire to boil her kettle and as soon as the fire reached the powder it went off with a loud retort and nearly blew the kettle up the chimney. After that people dreaded danger in burning charged stakes and they were allowed to remain in the hedges."

Eden Bank

Elliot memorial

"On a slight eminence near Wetheral stands the neat mansion of George Elliot called Eden Bank", stated Mannix & Whellan in their 1847 *Directory,* "delightfully situated nearly opposite Corby Castle and commanding fine views of the Scottish hills, Crossfell, etc. and the beautiful vale of the Eden." This they said, "was built in 1834 by Mr Elliot, who is tastefully ornamenting the grounds," but, as the house is not on the tithe map, a printing error may have transposed numbers and should have read 1843.

It was the first house to be built after the coming of the railway and so is an important property, as it led others to build there, developing the rest of the village. In the *Handbook of the Newcastle & Carlisle Railway* in 1851, Mr Elliot is referred to as "a merchant from Brampton" and in David Moorat's *Brampton Public Houses* details are given of 'Elliot's Spirit Vaults.'

The *Carlisle Patriot* 30 March 1861 advertised sites for building ground of one and three acres, adjoining Eden Bank, however on 7 October 1862 George Elliot died at Gilsland, before acquiring any neighbours.

According to the *Journal* "he had gone [there] in the hope of re-invigorating his failing constitution"; he was only 59. In his obituary the *Journal* stated, he was "reared in the wild regions of Liddlesdale where he acquired in boyhood a love for that legendary lore and ballad literature in which the district is so prolific; and with this he combined a taste for music that made his society ever a source of pleasure."

Mr Elliot was, said the newspaper, "a man of retired habits and quiet unobtrusive manner but nevertheless succeeded by his obliging disposition and genial manner in winning a larger share of esteem and respect than usually falls to the lot of men more actively engaged in public life." A substantial monument was erected in Wetheral churchyard recording his death and that of his only son aged two. Also recorded on the stone are George Elliot's in-laws, Jane and John Lawson. It was George Elliot's widow, Margaret, who continued at Eden Bank until her death on 3 March 1876. Aged only nine when his grandmother died, George Elliot Browning, later Chief Engineer for the Cochin Government 1896-1923, is supposed to have inherited the property, according to *Cumberland Families & Heraldry,* but it seems more likely to have been sold by trustees acting for the family.

The next occupant was James Steel, editor of the *Journal* and partner in the firm Steel Brothers of Carlisle, who lived there until September 1900, when he died aged 69. He was to be buried at Carlisle Cemetery and the *Journal* account of the funeral stated, "as it passed along the Plains the blinds of nearly all the houses were drawn as a mark of respect to one who had been an esteemed neighbour."

Eden Bank today

Commuting businessmen continued to favour this as a residence, William Boustead Oram of the Carlisle grocery firm, W Oram & Sons, was listed there in Bulmer's 1901 *Directory.* When W B Oram died in 1919 his place was taken by J H Oram and then in 1936 by, presumably his sister or daughter, Miss Emma Oram, who died in 1947.

Being a Carlisle family, all the Orams lie in Carlisle cemetery.

The Green

The grassed area in the centre of Wetheral was formerly common land which was enclosed along with the rest of Inglewood Forest in 1808. The future of the open space was threatened when it was offered for auction in 1814 by the Commissioners at Penrith. "Previous to the sale," said John Lawson in his reminiscences, "a meeting was held amongst the villagers, when it was resolved to purchase the Green and a deputation was appointed to attend the sale for that purpose."

"It was bid up to £30," stated Lawson, "when one of the villagers (not one of those deputed to buy, but one who had made too free a use of the whisky bottle) bid another £30 and at that figure it was knocked down."

Hurriedly a subscription list was opened, "and sufficient funds were soon raised in the village, with £10 from Henry Howard." With the necessary £60, "it then became the property of the villagers." The proviso was that it remained, "a free, open space to beautify the village and for free use of the inhabitants."

Henry Howard presented a larch tree which, "was dressed and painted and a weather cock was procured to place on top of it,

The cross on Wetheral Green

bearing the date of its erection, 1814, to be used as a Maypole." Some modifications were made to the Maypole, but after 30 years, "it began to show signs of decay and it was then thought desirable to have it taken down." Eventually (before 1838) a stone cross was erected to replace the Maypole and this is the one there today, in a less central location to allow games to be played on the green.

In 1925 there were complaints of what was happening to Wetheral on Sundays, "the quiet of Wetheral, which was, to visitors, almost as great a charm as the beauty of its setting, has departed with the arrival of the charabanc. Every Sunday and holidays it is a Mecca of pleasure-seekers and throughout the afternoon and evening the riverside, and the roadside and paths leading to it, are busy promenades". This "invasion of the village" and the resulting litter on the Green, was the subject of a meeting of the Parish Council in

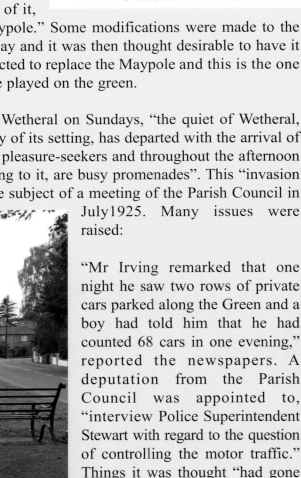

July 1925. Many issues were raised:

"Mr Irving remarked that one night he saw two rows of private cars parked along the Green and a boy had told him that he had counted 68 cars in one evening," reported the newspapers. A deputation from the Parish Council was appointed to, "interview Police Superintendent Stewart with regard to the question of controlling the motor traffic." Things it was thought "had gone too far".

Wetheral Green today with Wetheral Cross in the left background.

Oak Bank (Killoran)

A Cumrew farmer, John Scott of Albyfield and his wife Mary (nee Gibson) gave birth to a son, also John in 1811. This son lived to be 88 and in his *Journal* obituary it states, "he went to London in his boyhood, with the proverbial half - crown in his pocket, given him by his mother, and he became assistant in the warehouse in Cannon Street, of which he eventually became the head." The newspaper explained, "his career was one of great success and to his enterprise is mainly due the development of the famous Paisley shawl trade." He lived at Bickley in Kent in a house he called Albyfield, but also kept the farm in Cumbria of that name, with a tenant in residence. By 1869 he wanted a grander Cumbrian residence and so chose a site overlooking the church and village green at Wetheral.

Stained glass window on the stairs featuring the Scott coat-of-arms, by Messrs Heaton, Butler & Bayne, with the Latin motto 'Obstando supera'.

In March 1872 the completed building, then called Westerley House, was described in *The Architect* as having, "walls of red Dumfries sandstone with chimney pieces of white Fairloans stone, except that of marble in the drawing room; encaustic tiles in the hall by Messrs Maw and Co." The house was designed by the London architects Messrs Henry Javis and built by Thomas Nelson at a cost of £4000. It was designed, "as a personal indulgence to make a grand statement and very much with hospitality and enjoyment in mind," Mr Scott only came to the house in the autumn of each year. He seems to have preferred the name Oak Bank and it is marked as such on the second edition Ordnance Survey map in 1899.

When John Scott died, his son Alfred, who was vicar of St. Mary's Paddington, came to live at Oak Bank. The Rev. Scott soon found the house was too large for his needs and went to live at Albyfield, a house also facing the Green. He then let Oak Bank to Frank Carr, one of the directors of Carrs' Flour Mill Ltd. at Silloth. It seems that this tenant was responsible for the change of name to Killoran. The Rev Scott died in 1933 and Killoran was sold to Mrs Heslop who, by 1940, had opened the Killoran Nursing Home.

Keith Simmonds

John Scott J P

By 1952 John Sarginson was living there, but in July 1957 the house became the property of the Spadeadam Rocket Establishment. An advertisement in the *Cumberland News,* 1 April 1960, advertised vacancies at Killoran in the "Rocket Engine Department Branch Drawing Office". It seems that the house also boasted a hospitality suite at this time. The *Cumberland News* reported, "in that flamboyant period of its history Killoran played host to British and foreign dignitaries whenever they visited the research site."

In 1973 Killoran became surplus to requirements and was sold and by July 1975 it was called Killoran Guest House.

One year later it became the Killoran Country House Hotel. The hotel changed hands in 1981 and in 2007 the contents were sold at auction before conversion to luxury flats by A P & J Brown, retaining many of the original features.

Left: Killoran when it was a nursing home, about 1940.

Eden Mount

Eden Mount in 2008 showing the garden wall millstones which came from Newcastle.

This land was formerly known as The Croft, and was bought from William Robinson by Robert Anderson in January 1871 for £400. Mr Anderson was a native of Carlisle but from 1858 he spent, "the greater part of his life in China at Kin Kang in the service of Messrs Jardine, Mathieson & Co.," subsequently founding his own company as a tea merchant in London. Tenders were invited for a villa designed by John Hodgson of Carlisle and this was sufficiently advanced on 27 June 1871 for forty workmen to be invited, "to a supper at the Crown for the timber raising," stated the *Journal*. Kelly's *Directory,* 1873, lists Robert Anderson at Eden Mount, but he was rarely there and for that reason he sold it on 13 May 1876, for £3000, to his brother Thomas, a timber merchant of Denton Holme, where Anderson's still trades today.

Thomas lived there until 1881 when he had another house built, Oaklands (see page 46). From then on Eden Mount was the home of Thomas' unmarried sister Annie and his widowed mother, who died there in 1886 and 1888 respectively. A stained glass window in the church was erected to their memory.

The house was then bought again by Robert Anderson in 1890 and in 1892 he, living in London, sold to Mrs Mary Dunne (an heiress who had owned Tring Park before selling to the Rothschilds). She was married to John Dunne who, as Chief Constable for Cumberland and Westmorland, was knighted in 1897. Sir John died in 1906 and from then on there were a succession of owners, one being T R Cavaghan of the Carlisle bacon-curing firm of Cavaghan and Gray.

The *Journal* considered that with, "outer walls of fire bricks and corner stones of beautiful white stone, this was a great ornament to the village."

A change of ownership in 1912 resulted in millstones being added to the front garden wall. Many original features remain internally and this outstanding building was listed in 1993.

Carlisle Library

Above: Sir John Dunne. He lived at Eden Mount from 1892 to 1906. Mrs Carrick remembered him as, "tall, broad, stern and commanding."

J Wooliscroft

Right: Robert Anderson who commissioned the building of Eden Mount.

Left: Eden Mount in 1875.

J Wooliscroft

Lime House

Left: Lime House today.

Below: This photograph shows Lime House, originally built as two semi-detached houses.

Keith Simmonds

In the 1850s the daughters of Thomas Robinson, a Newcastle merchant, Elizabeth, Annie and Jane, decided to open a 'Ladies Boarding School' at Wetheral. The date is uncertain, but by 1856 they were advertising the school. In 1861 Elizabeth Robinson was head of household, aged 54, there being 30 girls in residence aged 13 and 14, many from the North East.

By 1871 the Robinsons had been replaced by Maria Nairn from Oldham, a widow aged 64 and her daughter Margaret. Both taught at what they called a Ladies Seminary and gave it the name Lime House. A varied curriculum was offered, two mistresses being engaged to teach German and French. Eventually Mrs Nairn decided to retire, and then "Miss Nairn's School continued there". On 2 September 1898 a formal notice appeared in the *Journal* advertising that the school, "carried on by Miss Nairn and her mother for 37 years would move to Englethwaite Hall near Armathwaite, which had been bought for the purpose." There the school remained until it closed in 1909.

In 1899 Mrs Crosthwaite, widow of a former headmaster of Carlisle Grammar School, took Lime House for a Boys Preparatory School, which she had previously run in Carlisle. She advertised that, "she prepares boys aged 6 - 14 for public schools". Later that year Mrs Crosthwaite erected a gymnasium at the rear. Such was her success that further extensions were made in 1917. In 1935, aged over 90, Mrs Crosthwaite reluctantly retired leaving H G Holman in charge. She then moved to Sussex to live with a daughter, where she died the following year.

In 1946 the school had outgrown Lime House and, taking the name with them, they moved to Holme Hill near Dalston, where the school flourishes to this day.

At some point Lime House had been purchased by Captain Dunne, a son of the late Sir John Dunne, (see opposite). In 1947 Captain Dunne sold the building to the Management Committee of the Cumberland Infirmary who "intended to use it as a nurses' home". This was a short term use before being purchased by the County Council as "a home for aged of both sexes". Lime House residential home continued until 1991 when it closed as an economy measure, despite opposition from local residents. Lime House is now the headquarters of the Cumbria Probation Service.

Left: Memorial stained glass window in Wetheral church given by past pupils of Mrs Nairn, founder of Lime House School.

Below: Detail of the inscription on the window.

TO THE GLORY OF GOD AND AS A TOKEN OF AFFECTION AND RESPECT ERECTED BY MANY OF HER PUPILS TO THE MEMORY OF MARIA NAIRN WHO DIED 8TH MARCH A D 1882 AGED 76 YEARS

Fantails

About 1953 Ellis and Marjorie Watson converted a 300 year old barn with filling station at Wetheral into a restaurant with living quarters. Lady Graham from Netherby performed the opening ceremony and the day's takings were donated to Wetheral Church. The Watsons are remembered for their innovative and sometimes eccentric ideas. An article in the *Cumberland News* in May 2002 recorded the memories of Lesley Norman of Wetheral, daughter of Les and Mary Ferguson who took over the restaurant in 1976:

"*Mam* Watson kept all sorts of birds on site including, of course, doves but also an arthritic Chinese goose called Sammy who killed three successive mates, but eventually took to a male Indian duck." She continued

Above: The Fantails before conversion to a restaurant.

Below: Partly converted. The 'Walls' sign was where ice-cream was served from a hatch to passers-by.

with more fascinating information, "Mrs Watson's living quarters had her bath raised about four feet from the floor with steps up to it and she stored a sliding bed under there which was pulled out for night time. In the restaurant she built a longcase clock into a pillar and a bureau in one of the recesses. They are still there to this day ... the mahogany double doors were salvaged from Hayton House ... the wrought iron bordering railings came from the old nunnery in Wetheral ... Fantails did not have a licence then and customers would have to dash across to the Crown to buy a bottle if they wanted alcohol ... diners were largely wealthy, including TV executives, race-goers ... people who owned boats and homes in the Lakes and families whose children were home from boarding school."

In 1976 all this changed when Mary and Les Ferguson and family took over. The Fantails had a reputation for being 'posh' but their motto was 'everybody is welcome'. "If they're paying money they all get treated the same." Lesley related an amusing incident about a visit from a Japanese prince to Fantails. "The police came first to check us out and the prince came with a taster. There was all this protocol about bowing and it was hilarious. We didn't know that he had to have the last bow so we kept on bowing after he did, until someone explained."

In 1988 the Fergusons gave up the business when Les took ill with cancer. Their son, Geoff, continued the catering tradition as chef at No. 10 restaurant in Stanwix. Sylvia Ingham (Cancer scanner fund raiser) took over for about 12 months, then Robert and Jenny Bowman (who had chemist shops in Carlisle) bought the Fantails. Since 1996 Kenny Hogg has run the business maintaining Les Ferguson's philosophy that Fantails is for everyone, but it is still popular with footballers and wealthy businessmen and has been visited by celebrities such as Robbie Williams and Kevin Keegan. He said, "We still have Pepi's room downstairs, named after Mrs Watson's pet monkey. Health and safety would have had a field day".

Below: A postcard of the Fantails as it was in the 1950s.

Below right: The Fantails today.

Keith Simmonds

Dorothy Carruthers

Keith Simmonds

The shop on the left, next down from the village hall, was a general grocers around 1900. John Smith, the man in the picture, was a part-time postman as well as delivering groceries for the shop. His daughter standing next to him is Agnes Smith. Agnes eventually took over the shop, which became know as Aggie's sweetshop, continuing in business until the 1940s.

Two doors further down the hill was J R Clark's butcher shop (left). Dorothy Carruthers writes "Robert Forster and his wife Mary (nee Peascod) had the butcher's shop in Wetheral in the early 1800s. Robert's son, John, married Jane Forsyth and soon after they went to Philadelphia. Later, on their return, they lived at the shop in Wetheral for a short time before opening a butcher's business in Carlisle under the Town Hall (1861 census)." John Forsyth, photographer, took this picture, probably in the 1890s, hence the change in name.

On the opposite side was Burrow's tailors and drapers shop. Thomas Burrow, the proprietor, was also a Methodist preacher (see page 11).

Next to the tailor's was the home and surgery of Dr Barclay, remembered for his 37 years service to the community on his gravestone in Wetheral cemetery.

Down from Dr Barclay's house was Mounsey's grocer. The sign also says 'apartments, accommodation for cyclists'

It is interesting also to note that directly opposite is Holly Cottage and on the gable end of the shed attached is a notice advertising 'cycles for hire' (this can be seen on the Bushby painting of Holly Cottage at the bottom of page 40).

Bottom right: The house and shop of Tom Burrows, tailor and Methodist preacher.

Below: Dr John Barclay with 'his man' John Jackson, (maternal grandfather to Keith Simmonds) behind his home, Anchor Lodge. The doctor would visit his outlying patients by horse and trap.

Keith Simmonds, both images

Corby Green

Right: A postcard looking east across part of the Green with the Forge on the left.

Great Corby Village Green has changed little over the years, being surrounded by some of the oldest buildings in the village.

In days gone by one crossed the Green on the way down to the ferry, but now it lies in a quiet cul-de-sac.

Ashley Kendall

Susan Bull

Left and above: 1977 saw the Green hosting a fair to celebrate the Queen's Jubilee, only one of many similar events on the Green over the years.

Mary Burgess

Above: William and Harriet Leslie, grandparents to Mary Burgess (nee Snowball), see page 69.

Mary Burgess

Left: William Leslie, bailiff at Corby Castle for thirty seven years supervising the allocation of wood to the inhabitants. This wood was stacked on the village green from where it was distributed to the locals.

Joe's Shop

Joe Armstrong

Left: Joe's shop which faced onto the village Green. It has now been converted into a private house.

Nigel Holmes wrote recently in the parish magazine about 'Joe's Shop'. "For 40 years everyone in Great Corby and beyond knew what those two words meant. For Joe Armstrong, now 85, has done more for his home area than most." He went on to describe how, on 20 November 1947, the Queen and the Duke of Edinburgh were married, as were Joe and Muriel Armstrong. Whilst still on their honeymoon Joe's father-in-law, Mr Steadman (a long established wholesale grocer in Carlisle), telephoned to say that the village shop in Great Corby was up for sale. Although Joe had already secured a position with Fisons Feeding Stuffs, he agreed the shop price including stock. Nigel continued, "Muriel's reaction was 'I swore I would never marry a grocer! You buy a shop without asking me.' As Joe says, 'I learned in one half-hour what being married meant. But Muriel was very supportive for the following forty years.' They rented Orchard House for £1 a week and kept hens in the back garden ... In those days there was also a butchers, Messrs Little and Steele, the milk round from Armstrong's farm, a joiner's shop in the forge (later a garage) as well as a bakery and post office/newsagent ... Joe quickly became popular, gaining customers from over the river and as far as Cumwhitton and Heads Nook ... he soon acquired the name 'The Midnight Grocer' ... he was rather late taking some orders ... altogether he had in excess of 50 weekly deliveries in addition to those who came to the shop." In 1953 Joe moved to Lyndale, his present home. He sold the shop 20 years ago but sadly Muriel died shortly afterwards.

Since then Joe has served the village as a parish councillor, taking particular interest in the playing field which he managed to extend and, until the last couple of years, cut the grass himself, as well as trimming the hedges (see page 84).

A gala day on the Green in 1960.

Peter Armstrong

Ashley Kendall

The forge at Great Corby. Joe's shop can be seen on the left.

The Queen Inn

Mary Burgess

Above: An earlier photograph of the house attached to the Queen Inn with Harriet Leslie at the door. Employees of the castle lived here.

Left: The Queen Inn today. The house above is now part of the Inn.

The Queen Inn, which faces onto the Green, can be dated back to 1776 when John Robinson was innkeeper and it was perhaps his death, recorded in 1820, aged 78. Then in 1829 the landlord, described as a "blacksmith/victualler" was named as William Robinson. In the 1841 census William was still in charge (aged 60) along with his wife Jane. In those days the inn was called The Queen Victoria. They were both still there in 1861 but on 16 September 1864 Jane died and by 1866 her son, John Robinson had taken over. The Robinson family continued at the inn until 1879 being replaced by George and Esther Christian until 1891, when the inn was described as The Queen for the first time. Landlords changed more frequently thereafter.

Communion Service at the Queen Inn

Cumbrian Newspapers

In recent years the inn has been used for meetings not normally associated with a public house. For example, on Sunday mornings in the 1990s Holy Communion was held in the inn for villagers who could not easily attend church at Wetheral; on the other side of the river.

The Queen Inn has been extended in recent years to include the cottage behind the inn and the house, above right, is now the restaurant. In the 1970s and 80s, when Judge's honey factory operated from the buildings behind the Queen Inn, this house was called Judge Cottage. The inn still gets a separate electricity bill for the restaurant addressed to Judge Cottage.

Carlisle Library

Right: This painting of the Queen Inn and Corby Green, seen from the forge, is by John Robinson, landlord of the Inn from 1866 to about 1872.

Corby Bridge Inn

Joe Armstrong

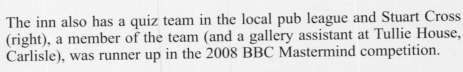

CORBY BRIDGE INN SPORTS.

ROBERT HARDING begs to intimate to his friends and the Public in general, that he intends having his Annual PIGEON SHOOTING, on EASTER MONDAY, APRIL 13th, 1857, when the following prizes will be given to contend for, viz:—

£2. to be Shot for at Pigeons, with 2s. 6d. entrance added to the prize. To be shot at with 1½ oz., of shot, 21 yards from the trap; the gun to lay on a rest till the bird is on the wing. Any person shooting at another man's bird before it has fairly passed the boundary line to be fined 5s.

£2. to be run for by horses that never won ten pounds, (matches excepted.) Three to start or the added money will be withheld. To be run on green turf.

10s. for the losing horses, 10s. to trot for, and 5s. for Donkeys.

All disputes to be settled by the Stewards.

N.B.—500 Pigeons wanted at 1s per couple.

A Ball in the evening, and Dinner on the table as usual.

Above: Advert for the annual 'sports' at the inn where 500 pigeons were needed as targets (before the days of clay pigeon shooting).

Left: Corby Bridge hotel when James Beavan was the landlord in 1905.

Lower left: A fireplace tile in the Inn of a type used by Harry Redfern, architect to the State Management Scheme.

On 13 July 1836 Henry Brooke made a journey along the Newcastle & Carlisle Railway as far as Greenhead. This was a week before the line opened and his account describing the route was published by Thurnams soon afterwards. Brooke described Corby Bridge and said, "a little beyond the eastern end, a new and commodious inn has been erected by Mr T Wannop." This was known as the Corby Bridge Inn but sometimes it was called an hotel and occasionally the Fox and Hounds.

Tenants came and went, at first being run by William and Jane Lawson and then Robert Harding until 1876. From then on the changes were more regular, the inn being acquired by the Old Brewery in 1898. Thus, on the takeover of the breweries by the Central Control Board in 1916, Corby Bridge Inn became a house tied to the Carlisle Brewery. Annual sports were held here by Robert Harding in the 1850s and in 1911 James Beavan advertised he was to open a "dogs home and infirmary ... at moderate charges at the Corby Bridge Hotel."

In more recent times the Corby Bridge Inn has been the home of Great Corby football team which was started in 1998 by Ian Nelson and was sponsored by John Delap, father to Premier Division footballer Rory Delap (see page 90). John Delap is now manager of the club, which has grown and progressed very well. Stephen Bell and Nigel North are now the club's main sponsors backed up by the Bridge Inn.

The team is seen below in April 2008, about to play a home game on Great Corby recreation ground. Left, an exciting excerpt from a match on the Sheepmount at Carlisle against the Milbourne Arms.

The inn also has a quiz team in the local pub league and Stuart Cross (right), a member of the team (and a gallery assistant at Tullie House, Carlisle), was runner up in the 2008 BBC Mastermind competition.

Back row left to right: Ian Nelson, Richard Ellwood, Simon Broatch, Gary McReidy, Felix Crawley, Mark Irvine, Phil Smith, Dave Mason and John Delap.

Front row left to right: Graham Farish, Kelvin Broatch, Steven Ellwood, Ben Hastings, Lex Crawley, Mark McReidy and John Graham.

Hawthorn Cottage

FRED DALTON

Hawthorn Cottage was originally two dwellings, which probably explains its L shape, and was a bakery at one time. Nigel Holmes relates how he bought the cottage in 1972 from, "Sir Ian Godfrey Bosville MacDonald of Sleat, 17th Baronet created 1625; Premier Baronet of Nova Scotia; 25th Chief of Sleat, who is only 60 but succeeded his father as a child. He now lives in East Yorkshire."

Nigel also described another previous occupant who was quite a character, a batchelor called Fred Dalton, "Frank Lawson, our next door neighbour when we came here, painted a number of men who drank in the Queen Inn. The pictures hung in the pub. When they died the pictures were given to their widows but Fred's came to the cottage. We passed the picture on with the cottage when we sold it in 1986 to the Simpsons, who still live there. The story goes that Fred is pictured holding a tankard, which was a rare point in time because he was not noted for his generosity, and with a tankard people could not see when it was empty!"

Dorothy Carruthers

Mrs Campling

Above: This photograph (circa 1900) by John Forsyth shows Hawthorn Cottage when it was thatched and consisted of two dwellings.

Right: Hawthorn Cottage in the process of being renovated, re-roofed and converted into one dwelling.

Incidentally Nigel Holmes now lives at Woodside, Great Corby. Nigel, before retirement, was well known as a presenter for Radio Cumbria. It is interesting to note that the previous owner of Woodside was Derek Batey who made his name at Border Television in the seventies with his Mr and Mrs Show. Prior to that an Olympic swimmer lived there and the original owner was a commercial artist at Hudson Scott, one William Gibson, described in the 1901 census as a Graphic Artist, Designer. He was a colleague of John Forsyth who lived next door at Aglionby House (see pages 44 and 45).

The Norval Murder

The rather morbid postcard below was on sale in Carlisle in 1911 to commemorate a sensational murder case at the time. The victim, Alexander Norval (75 years old), happened to live in Great Corby at the old schoolhouse, Brook Villa. He was a currier (i.e. he dressed and coloured tanned leather) at his business premises, a warehouse, 15 West Walls, where he worked with his son, Archibald. On 5 November 1910 a policeman on his rounds found the door of the premises unlocked and entered to discover Mr Norval lying dead in a pool of blood at the bottom of the stairs. His son lived nearby in Carlisle, a few minutes walk from West Walls. Archibald's excited behaviour when told of the death, the fact that he was intoxicated and other evidence about how his father kept Archibald short of money and worked him very hard, led the police to suspect that the old man had been murdered by his son. Archibald was duly brought to trial by jury at the Cumberland Assizes accused of parricide.

The trial, which lasted three days, attracted much interest. On 31 January 1911 the *Journal* reported that on the third day, "The Court was crowded and hundreds of people stood outside all day, unable to get in ... After about a quarter of an hour's deliberation the jury returned into Court with a verdict of Not Guilty and the judge at once ordered his discharge from custody. The announcement of the verdict was received with cheers both in the Court and the streets outside."

As a result of the scandal caused and notwithstanding the fact that Archibald had been acquitted, Stanwix Bowling Club Committee resolved to strike him from their membership list. The *Journal* reported "Mr Norval challenged the legality of this action and instituted an action against the club."

This resulted in the club backing down and paying Mr Norval's costs. He then undertook to resign his membership.

[Photo by Tassell.
THE PRISONER, ARCHIBALD NORVAL.

STANWIX BOWLING CLUB.

THE THREATENED ACTION BY MR. ARCHIBALD NORVAL.

AN ARRANGEMENT EFFECTED.

At the annual meeting of the Stanwix Bowling Club some weeks ago, it was resolved to strike off the membership roll the name of Archibald Norval, who was tried and acquitted on the charge of murdering his father at the last Cumberland Assizes. Mr. Norval challenged the legality of the club's action, and instituted an action against the club.

We understand that negotiations between Messrs. Halton and Hodgson, acting for Mr. Archibald Norval, and Messrs. Saul and Lightfoot, acting for the Stanwix Bowling Club, have resulted in the termination of the proceedings on the terms of the Club paying Mr. Norval's costs and acknowledging Mr. Norval as a member of the Club. Mr. Norval undertakes to now resign his membership.

THE LATE
MR A NORVAL
AT HIS HOME

- MURDERED - NOV. 5TH 1910 -

Keith Simmonds

Wetheral in Literature

First mentioned in *Tinsley's Magazine* for November 1869, in an article on Wetheral, was the suggestion that "De Quincey lived there once and wrote there a romance, *The Stranger's Grave,"* which had previously been anonymous. This was also the subject of a letter in the *Times Literary Supplement* in 1920 by J Scott Duckers giving evidence that Richard De Quincey at one time lived in Wetheral and was visited there by his brother Thomas. The correspondent's father, James Samuel Duckers, had recently purchased some property in Wetheral for which the deeds showed in 1814 a "Mansion House and Garth" (which today is Eden Croft) was sold by a "Thomas Latimer of Wetheral, Carpenter" for £250 to "Richard De Quincey, gentleman". The cottage was then re-conveyed by De Quincey in 1816 to a "William Elliott of Wetheral, shoemaker," the price then being £290 (see opposite).

In the letter "Mr Duckers mentions that Mr Howard of Corby Castle remembers being told by his father that Thomas De Quincey lived in the house in question and also wrote an idyll about the Boat Pool in the river. Mr Howard's grandfather is said to have once visited De Quincey to ask him to dine at the castle, but being a shy man, the essayist refused."

Above: The 1988 reprint of *The Stranger's Grave* acknowledging (for the first time) Thomas De Quincey as author.

Mr Duckers knew of the attribution of *The Stranger's Grave* to De Quincey and says of Richard De Quincey that, "after an adventurous life at sea, he purchased the cottage at Wetheral in 1814, but soon tired of rural life and resumed his travels."

The Stranger's Grave was published in 1823 and was set partly in Wetheral. In his book *The Opium Eater,* Grevel Lindop said that he thinks *The Stranger's Grave* was written while De Quincey was visiting his brother in 1814 and 1815 and, "it seems probable that the novel was De Quincey's work, but unless new evidence comes to light we may never be quite certain." As the novel begins with a description of Wetheral in the early 19th century it is worth giving this in full:-

"There are few situations, even in the romantic county of Cumberland, more strikingly picturesque and beautiful than that in which the village of Wetheral stands. It is built along the side of a hill, from the summit of which a fine and extensive prospect of hill and valley, wood and water, meets the eye; but being itself somewhat beneath the ridge, he who looks forth from amidst its white-washed and unassuming cottages, finds his gaze is compressed within much narrower limits. At the base of this hill, along a channel which seems as if it had been formed by some sudden convulsion of nature, runs the river Eden; not smoothly and quietly like the rivers of the south, but chafing and roaring from pool to pool, or dashing over the broken ledges of rock, which at innumerable intervals arise to interrupt its progress. The bank upon which Wetheral hangs, is, comparitively bare of foliage. Somewhat higher up the stream, indeed , the woods thicken on this side as well as on the other; but it is upon the opposite bank, overshadowed with the tall trees for which the grounds of Corby Castle are remarkable, that the eye of the spectator is irrestistibly enchained. The bank upon which Corby Castle stands, rises, like that of Wetheral, to a considerable height above the stream. Here art and nature seem to have done their utmost to produce a scene of unrivalled beauty, and it must be confessed that they have not laboured in vain. The whole face of the hill is covered with the most luxuriant wood, through which are cut narrow winding footpaths, intercepted ever and anon by some tall red rock, or ending in the mouth of a cave hewn out in the side of the cliff. Rich groves descend from the very crown of the hill to the margin of

Wetheral in Literature

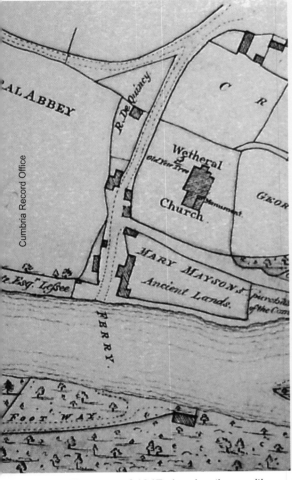

Cumbria Record Office

the river, insomuch that the branches of the weeping willows and other recumbent trees are kept in continual motion by the running of the stream; whilst their order is so admirably irregular, that all appearance of art is entirely kept out of sight. Like other mountain streams, the river Eden is winding in its course. At this place the curve is such as to place the lowermost cottages of Wetheral within a perfect ampitheatre of hills; the high banks closing in to both the right and left, so rapidly as to reduce the whole compass of the prospect within the space of perhaps a mile in length and little more than a bowshot in breadth. But to the real lover of nature, a scene like this can hardly be too confined. In the rich, wide, fertile, and unbroken plains of the south, such a one feels himself one of the crowd - a being who moves and must continually move under the gaze of the world: but in the narrow glens and vales of the north, he is alone. His eye takes in all of earthly things which it desires to embrace, - the clear glassy stream, the incumbcut rock, and the hanging wood; whilst even the blue sky appears more beautiful, because it is not boundless. The village of Wetheral consists of a church, remarkable for its neatness and simplicity; a vicarage house close by, embosomed in the shrubs which adorn its paddock and garden; a little inn or public house distinguished by the picture of a cart-wheel which dangles from the bough of a tree by the door, and somewhere about a dozen cottages. These are scattered in irregular order along the hillside, only the church and parsonage crowning the summit."

Above: The map of 1817 showing the position of the De Quincey property opposite the church.

Below: An 1860s view down Church Brow towards the ferry showing the church gate (left) and directly opposite Eden Croft. From the upper-floor window where the girl poses, it would be possible to look into the churchyard and see the stranger's grave.

(1) There is an agreement dated August 24, 1814, made between "Thomas Latimer of Wetheral, Carpenter," and "Richard De Quincey of the same, Gentleman," for sale to the latter of what was called a "Mansion House and Garth" (but was in feality a small cottage) for the sum of £250. This document bears the signatures "Thos. Latimer" and "Richd. de Quincey," and was witnessed by Isaac Hudson, Deputy Steward of the Manor of Wetheral, the property being then (and now) of customary tenure under the Dean and Chapter of Carlisle.

(2) A formal conveyance of the property dated June 3, 1815, to Richard de Quincey bears the signature and seal of Thomas Latimer only, and there is a copy of the admittance of Richard de Quincey on the Court Roll.

(3) The property was reconveyed by deed dated May 28, 1816, and made between Richard de Quincey, Gentleman, of the one part, and William Elliott of Wetheral, Shoemaker, of the other part —the consideration being £290. This deed bears the signature "Richd. de Quincey" opposite a plain seal, and a receipt for the purchase money is indorsed and signed by the vendor.

Above: Details given by James Scott Duckers of his father's deeds for Eden Croft in the *Times Literary Supplement*.

Carlisle Library

Sam Bough at Wetheral

Sam Bough (1822–1878) is one of Carlisle's most important 19th century artists. Bough was born on the 8 January 1822 in Atkinson's Court off Abbey Street, Carlisle, the third of five children. This building has long since been demolished but a plaque dated 1896 marks the spot. Although he moved away Sam retained strong links with the city throughout his highly successful career as an artist.

On display at Torquay in Torre Abbey Historic House & Art Gallery is *A Shady Lane near Wetheral*, 1842, by Sam Bough. This is a large oil painting and is perhaps one of his earliest canvasses. Wetheral is where he developed his technique in oils and this is confirmed by the *Carlisle Patriot,* which in October 1861 said, "Sam Bough has been for some time staying at Wetheral sketching some of the beautiful scenery where years ago he found the subject of many of his earliest productions."

Fortunately, in 1894 (21 August), a correspondent sent to the *Journal* a series of recollections in which he reminisced, "There are few now living, perhaps I am the only one, who were occasionally present and had some of the hospitality of Sam Bough at Wetheral." He continued, "early in the forties Sam pitched his tent in the field by the side of the Eden, through which you pass on the way to the cells ... and here he lived and painted and entertained and was lionised for nearly a couple of months. He was attended and waited on in all his merry humours by Jemmy [he was in fact called John], a thin old man, an old soldier who had been at Waterloo and was pensioned. Jemmy, like his master, was a bit of a character. It was the height of summer and in the evenings Sam's camp was a great draw-up place for the folks."

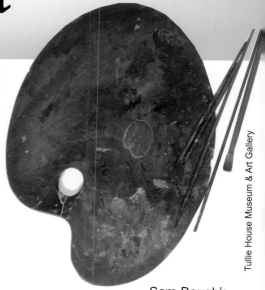

Tullie House Museum & Art Gallery

Sam Bough's palette and brushes.

Carlisle Library

John McDougall, Bough's companion, oil on canvas by Sam Bough.

Tullie House Museum & Art Gallery

Tullie House Museum & Art Gallery

Sam Bough aged 24, 1846, watercolour by William Percy.

Left: View of the River Eden showing Wetheral Church, bridge and ferry, about 1845, oil on canvas by Sam Bough.

As the recipient of a Waterloo medal, John Mc Dougall would have proudly worn this each year on 18 June, the anniversary of the battle.

Denis Perriam

Tullie House Museum & Art Gallery

Wetheral Ferry about 1870, watercolour by Sam Bough.

Sam Bough at his easel late in life.

Carlisle Library

The correspondent explained that the field was part of the Wetheral Abbey farm of Fergus Graham and he used to supply all the butter, eggs, milk and vegetables required for the camp. Every night there was a fiddler and another local played the cornet.

"There was dancing and singing till late and Jemmy used to brew coffee and pass it round." said the correspondent. He went on to describe Sam's outfit. "His get up was grand navvy boots, white stockings, black velveteen knee breeches, a big velveteen coat like a gamekeeper's, a nonedescript waistcoat, a great display of white shirt, a black tie, somewhat Byronic, a top hat and a large display of jewellery."

In response to this William Farish wrote from Chester (4 September), "The reference to Sam Bough's encampment about the year 1844 or 1845 was especially refreshing for I remember all concerning it and was well acquainted as well with the budding artist as with his man Friday, John - not Jemmy - McDougall. They were both characters in their own way, not easily forgotten." Mr Farish confirmed, "Your correspondent very accurately describes the personal oddities of Sam and those of John were almost as singular, if not quite so conspicuous."

Thomas Bushby

Below: A pastural scene looking towards Wetheral Church, a watercolour probably painted during World War I.

Ashley Kendall, both images

Flowers not Sown by Human Hands.
Thos. Bushby 1903

Above: 'Flowers not sown by human hands' painted in 1903 in Wetheral Woods and produced as a Thurnam postcard. These were the Adams children of High Croft Farm.

Thomas Bushby (1861-1918) was obviously delighted by the scenery around Wetheral from the number of works he painted there. He returned over a number of years, probably visiting on his way, John Forsyth (see page 44), a colleague at the Metal Box firm of Hudson Scott and a close friend.

Thos Bushby 1907

Tullie House Museum & Art Gallery

Above: Cottages at Wetheral, painted in 1907.
This was a printer's proof but seems never to have been published.

Denis Perriam

Right: Holly Cottage, Wetheral, painted in 1907 and printed as a postcard by Thurnams in their cottage series. At the gate is Mrs Lancaster and on the road is Mrs Whittaker with her daughter and dog called Richmond.

Visiting Artists

Right: William James Blacklock (1816-1854) was born at Cumwhitton so Wetheral was very familiar to him. He began a series of lithographic views along the N&C Railway, but got no further than two before the scheme was abandoned. Had he drawn the railway the prints may have sold more successfully. Here he chose the ruins of the abbey (priory) rather than the viaduct.

Carlisle Library

Below: A whole series of pencil drawings were made by J W Carmichael of Corby Bridge in 1835. These and other drawings done at the same time formed the basis of his very successful *Views on the Newcastle and Carlisle Railway* published in 1839.

Tullie House Museum & Art Gallery

Lower left: Like other artists Matthew Nutter was fascinated by the enormity of Corby Bridge and returned on a number of occasions to depict the scene. This engraving of 1836 made his work more available.

Below: Much influenced by W J Blacklock, W J Fairlie (1825-1875) visited the same locations and produced similar views. A number of watercolours of Wetheral were exhibited by Fairlie at Thurnams in 1863. This oil painting is one of his masterpieces.

John Parker

Carlisle Library

Resident Artists

Both Wetheral and Great Corby could boast talented resident artists who were either natives or had settled there. Some were obvious off-comers, their names suggesting European origins. One example is Frank Bertioli who was listed on the 1901 census as a portrait artist of Great Corby, then aged 67. His birthplace was given as Middlesex and he had exhibited at Tullie House in 1896 from a Great Corby address. While the census gives his wife's name as Caroline, the *Carlisle Patriot* records the death of Catherine Bertioli at Great Corby in 1908 aged 63.

A teacher of French and a native of that country, Arthur Cornillon, frequently came to Wetheral to give private lessons. His artistic abilities were apparent from a lithographic view of Carlisle in 1832. When he went to Whitehaven to give classes in 1846 he advertised that he had resided in Carlisle for 14 or 15 years. But it was at Great Corby that he was discovered dead. An inquest on 12 February 1847 found that he fell from Corby Bridge hitting a buttress on his descent to the river. The jury returned a verdict, "that the deceased was found dead but there was not sufficient evidence to show whether it was a case of suicide or otherwise."

Dorothy Smithson

Above: The Last Look by Frank Bertioli, a pastel portrait of Mary Pigg at Fern Bank, Great Corby, dated 16 July 1899.

Another with a foreign-sounding name was George Blake Hildebrande, but he was born at Beverley, East Yorkshire. His lithograph of Wetheral Church in the 1840s is seen on page 9. In 1841 he was living at Eden Holme on Station Road. With his mother born in Bath and with no employment, George Hildebrande would seem to have been of private means. He never married and remained with his sister and mother, the family moving first to Lazonby by 1851, Pooley Bridge by 1861 and Red Hills near Penrith by 1867, where the whole family died in the same year, George aged 67.

An exhibition of 60 watercolours by Mrs F J Rose was held at Church House, Carlisle in 1919, the newspaper giving her address as Pallazza Moroni, Rome and Upna House, Wetheral. Some of the scenes exhibited were of Wetheral and others were Italian. The *Journal* stated, "she studied under Signor Nardi in Rome, a famous artist and frequently exhibited in London."

In an obituary of John Milburn, who died at Hexham in August 1901, his birthplace was given as Great Corby. He was described as a good sculptor, had lived at Hexham for 15 years and died aged 40.

Michael Finlay

Of the many amateur artists Henry Moss was the most unlikely, being a pawnbroker from Carlisle. He came to live at Fern Bank House at Wetheral Pastures in 1878 and painted many scenes around Wetheral. His obituary in the *Journal* gives his death in November 1910 aged 84.

Left: The Wheatsheaf at Wetheral by Henry Moss, dated 1885. This was one of a number of watercolours painted by the artist of Wetheral and Great Corby.

Photographers

For generations many of the photographs taken professionally in the area were by Joseph Spottiswood Farrer. He was originally from Walton where his father, John, was a husbandman on a farm.

Aged 31 and already a photographer, Joseph married Mary Nixon, a farmer's daughter, on 17 March 1892 at Lanercost and then moved to Wetheral. They had three children. One of his two daughters Florence (born 1896), wrote to the *Cumberland News* in 1961.

"J S Farrer, photographer of Brampton and Wetheral was my father. He was born in 1860 and died in 1952. He would own one of the first bicycles in Cumberland and he cycled to his photographer's business in Brampton, three days every week for over thirty years." Mary had died by 1901 and Joseph re-married at Wetheral to Jane Noble of Great Corby, the daughter of a railway fenceman. They lived for many years at Edenside, Wetheral.

Keith Simmonds

Above: Joseph Farrer was quite a sportsman, seen here in a self-portrait photograph after a successful day's shooting.

Right: Each carte-de-visit photograph (so named as it was the size of a visiting card) which Farrer took, had an elaborate back advertising the days his studio in Brampton and Wetheral were open.

Below: The Farrer family outside their home, Edenside.

Keith Simmonds

Liz Hodgson

Dorothy Carruthers

Left: The quality of Farrer's work is seen in this photograph of the wedding of Clara Forsyth to John Muirhead. It was taken in front of Aglionby House, Great Corby on 28 May 1912.

John Forsyth

Dorothy Carruthers (all images)

Aglionby House, Great Corby, was, until 1915, the home of John Forsyth, designer, commercial artist and keen photographer. He was one of the founder members of the Carlisle and District Photographic Society (1886). Although born in Carlisle John moved to London and Glasgow in childhood and eventually came to live in Broad Street. His father, an artist and designer, had taken a job at Hudson Scott. This firm, one of the foremost in the production of lithographically decorated tin boxes, employed many artists in the area and attracted others here.

John also was taken on by Hudson Scott and worked twenty two years for them. During this time he had a house built in Aglionby Street. Later he had another house built at Great Corby, which he named Aglionby House. John's son, Harold, was also a talented artist and when he tragically died, early in 1910, his mother could no longer bear to live in Great Corby and they decided to move to Kelsick Moss House, Abbeytown.

Above: John Forsyth's photograph above of the drawing room in Aglionby House gives a good idea of how a Victorian drawing room was furnished at the end of the 19th century. His granddaughter, Dorothy Carruthers, still has items of furniture from this room.

Below: Aglionby House, Great Corby, built in 1896 for John Forsyth. Members of the Forsyth family stand in the garden.

Above: In 1900 John Forsyth became a freelance designer and moved to Aglionby House, where he built a large studio in his garden.

John Forsyth

An illuminated address to Judge and Mrs Hills, Corby Castle, Great Corby. June 16, 1902.

John's studio, along with his tools, equipment, and household effects were transported to Abbeytown on a large pantechnicon, hauled by a traction engine.

At Brookfield, near Wigton, the railway bridge partly collapsed with the weight but, eventually, they got there.

As a freelance John worked for many different organisations and individuals including Thurnams and Carlisle City Council. Several of the illuminated addresses in the Dormant book in Carlisle are the work of John Forsyth.

An example of his design work from 1902 is shown left, being an illuminated address from the villagers to Judge and Mrs Hills, the tenants at that time of Corby Castle, who were giving up their tenancy.

Other important commissions were illuminated addresses for Woodrow Wilson, the American President who was on a pilgrimage to his mother's birthplace and Prince Christian of Schleswig Holstein, on his visit to the city.

Mrs J Forsyth was very friendly with Mrs Hills. When Clara Forsyth married John S Muirhead, Mrs Hills gave her a permanent pass to the grounds of Corby Castle for her family. John exhibited his photographs in Carlisle's first museum in Finkle Street before Tullie House became the venue of the Carlisle and District Photographic Society annual exhibitions. John Forsyth died in 1934 aged 79.

Below: This illuminated address by John Forsyth was given to Mr and Mrs Hudson Scott from the firm of Hudson Scott to commemorate the occasion of their Golden Wedding. The miniature portraits are on ivory and the scroll is in Tullie House Museum.

Dorothy Carruthers

Below: This sketch of Corby Green was made by John Forsyth, circa 1900, in the autograph book of Mary Elizabeth Pigg, mother of Dorothy Smithson.

Dorothy Smithson

"There's no prettier Village you could name" than Great Corby

Houses

Cumbria Record Office

Left: Oaklands viewed from Plains Road dating from 1881 and built for Thomas Anderson (above).

Below: Mooryeat was the home of J H Martindale.

Cumberland News 18 April 1958

Above: A native of Chester, J H Martindale had come to Carlisle from an architectural practice in Leeds. When only 20 he had won the first prize of the Architectural Association of Ireland for a town church. He was highly regarded in his profession and was President of the Northern Architectural Association.

In 1881 Thomas Anderson, who was already living in Wetheral at Eden Mount (see page 26), wanted a new house and engaged C J Ferguson to design Oaklands. Thomas had been in partnership with James Graham as timber merchants in Denton Holme, Carlisle, but when Graham left it became Anderson and Sons. A daughter, Isabel, had married Richard Rigg MP and it was at their house in London that both Thomas and his wife, Hannah, died. However they were buried at Wetheral.

Another prominent family in the village were the Martindales. James Henry Martindale had come to Carlisle as an assistant to C J Ferguson, eventually setting up his own architectural practice. His speciality was church architecture and he was architect to Carlisle Cathedral, where on his death in 1931 he was succeeded by his son C J F Martindale and then his grandson C B Martindale.
J H Martindale designed many houses in the area, one being his own house, Mooryeat.

Estates

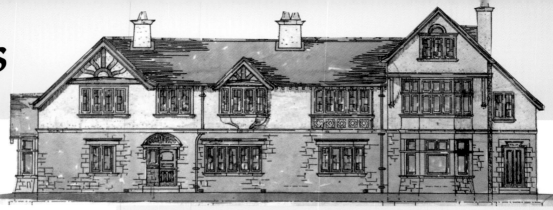

SEMI-DETACHED HOUSES FAUSTIN HILL ESTATE, FOR THE MISSES BEATTIE.

Cumbria Record Office

FAUSTIN HILL
GREENACRES

Faustin Hill and Greenacres estates use the original field names

WETHERAL BUILDING SOCIETY.

DECEMBER 3RD, 1839.

THE following Resolutions were passed at a Meeting, held this Day, in the School Room, at Scotby, ELIHU SUTTON in the Chair.

1st. Resolved—"That a Society be Established called the PARISH of WETHERAL BUILDING SOCIETY, which shall be formed as soon as 50 Shares are Subscribed for."

2nd. Resolved—"That the amount of each Share be £120, at a subscription of Ten Shillings per month, and that none be allowed to have less than One Share, or more than Six."

Individuals intending to become Shareholders, will please attend to the above Time and Place, or leave there names at

Mr. J. D. CARR, or   } Carlisle.
Mr. ROBERT BEND   }

Mr. WM. SUTTON, jun., or } Scotby.
Mr. WM. WANNOP,   }

By any of whom any further information will be given.

An early application is necessary as about 30 Shares were subscribed for at the Meeting, and the number will be limited.

JOHN WRIGHT, Sec. Pro. Tem.

There were attempts to build affordable housing for the working classes, a Wetheral Building Society being established in 1840. But most of what was on offer was for the more wealthy. Semi-detached villas were planned in 1904 at Faustin Hill but the scheme got no further than two houses (above and below).

Newspapers complained in 1925 that there were no council houses and a need for, "new dwellings, especially for young married people ... attributing the falling birth-rate to the housing problem". Nothing was done, the District Council pointing out they, "were prepared to give all possible financial assistance to private enterprise under the Act of 1923." Post-war attitudes changed and Mrs Kirkpatrick said twenty two houses were built by the County and Border Rural Councils, "on the field called 'Faustin' .... in the possession of the Wetheral Parish Council." Since this 1950s development other private houses have been built, adopting field names for estates where appropriate.

Wandales (Geltsdale)

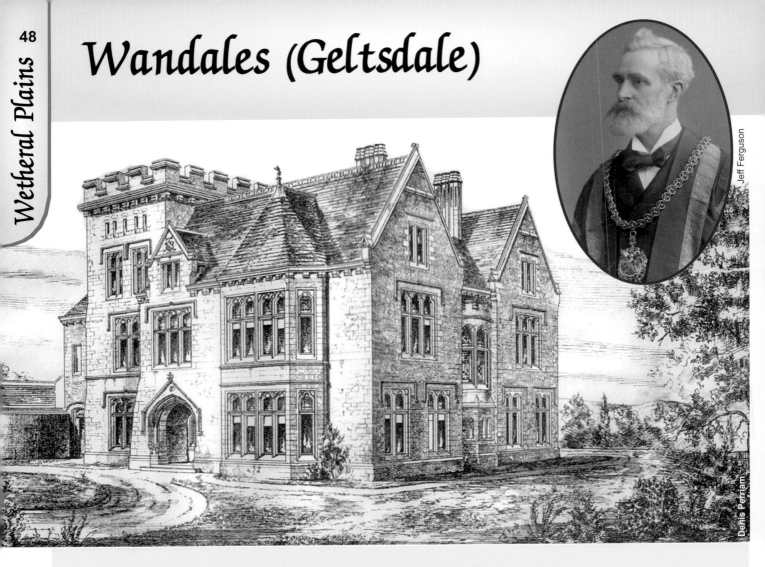

Jeff Ferguson

Denis Perriam

An architect's drawing (above) by George Dale Oliver, of the firm Hetherington and Oliver of Carlisle, for the proposed house 'Wandale, Cumberland', appeared in *The Building News* 11 November 1881. This was the design for a house being built for Christopher Ling, a corn merchant in Carlisle and future mayor of the city (inset above).

According to Prescott the house name came from, "Anglo-saxon *wang* 'an open field' or 'plain' and *doel* 'a share,' a division of the open arable field of a village or township." Built as shown, the only alteration to the plan was the addition of a 's' to the name, and this was where the Ling family lived for over 20 years. After the death of Mr Ling's second wife in 1904 he could no longer bear to live at Wandales and put the house up for sale, moving to Birkdale, Southport with his daughter.

The illustrated catalogue for the auction of the property in 1905 stated "the situation is unrivalled in well sheltered grounds on an elevated plateau, from every room delightful views." This, said the *Journal,* was "built of stone in a style unsurpassed anywhere." However the house failed to meet its reserve (it had cost over £5000 to build) and was let the following year to F C Bolton. He remained in residence until 1913 (the year before Mr Ling died) when the house was again offered for sale. In May the *Journal* reported that the first bid of £7,100 was below the reserve, but the house was sold privately to Jacob Vickers of Holywood Hall, Wolsingham, County Durham, for an undisclosed sum. Mr Vickers died in 1923 but his widow remained in residence.

A sale of surplus furniture from Wandales in 1925 suggests a change in ownership. Kelly's *Directory* records Mrs Mary Isabella Vickers as being there at that time and in 1934 Hugh Hodgson was in residence. At some point before World War II the name changed to 'Geltsdale.' Miss A H P Linton lived there in 1940 and that year saw a change, Margaret Kirkpatrick saying, "Geltsdale was requisitioned by the Air

Right: Wandales as it was when the Ling family lived there.

Keith Simmonds

Ministry for a wing of the Administration." From then on the house was known as RAF Wetheral, part of 50 Wing. It was used as a duplicate communications centre for the delivery of aircraft from maintenance to operational units. This was felt necessary in case of enemy bombing. "But," said Mrs Kirkpatrick, "before the war ended they were transferred to other quarters and Geltsdale was turned into a hostel for the Women's Land Army [see page 70]."

From the late forties Geltsdale House became a County Council orphanage before West Cumberland Farmers took it over. In 1983 Eden Construction purchased the property and, when an application to develop the site was refused, a public enquiry was held. The house remains externally as built but has now been converted into domestic accommodation.

The last surviving child of Christopher Ling, Lt Col Robert Welton Ling, died in London in December 1967, aged 81, and his request was that his ashes were to be interred at Wetheral Cemetery where other members of the family are buried.

Jeff Ferguson

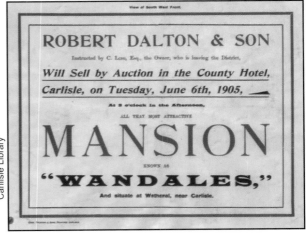

Carlisle Library

Left: Mrs Ling when Mayoress in 1900, whose death prompted the sale of Wandales.

Above right: Wandales Lodge on Plains Road which was at the entrance to the house.

Right: The auction notice for the sale in 1905.

View of South West Front.

ROBERT DALTON & SON

Instructed by C. Lin, Esq., the Owner, who is leaving the District,

Will Sell by Auction in the County Hotel, Carlisle, on Tuesday, June 6th, 1905,

At 3 o'clock in the Afternoon,

ALL THAT MOST ATTRACTIVE

MANSION

KNOWN AS

"WANDALES,"

And situate at Wetheral, near Carlisle.

Newcastle & Carlisle Railway

CORBY BRIDGE.
FRANCIS GILES. CIVIL ENGINE
WILLIAM DENTON BUILDER
MDCCCXXXI. MDCCCXXXIII

As early as January 1826 the *Journal* featured a letter about the possible site of a bridge over the River Eden for the new railway. The route had to be reasonably level and pass through countryside where there were compliant landowners, but the Earl of Carlisle demanded it to be out of site of Naworth Castle.

As a director of the railway however, Henry Howard of Corby Castle, was open to persuasion. When the railway was to pass close to his castle, he could see this as an asset to the landscape. Sarah Losh of Woodside, near Wreay, suggested, "a bridge similar to the Pont du Gard, a few miles from Nimes, as calculated to harmonise well with the lofty banks of the river and the exquisitely wooded scenery of Corby Castle and made drawings of her proposed plan that found acceptance with Mr Howard." It was left to Francis Giles, as architect to the company, to come up with the final design.

In June 1829 a cottage and garden were advertised to be let, "close to the place where the bridge for the

Above: Corby Bridge, usually described as Wetheral Viaduct, by Matthew E Nutter, watercolour, 1835. Artistic licence has allowed the removal of the m

Below: Corby Beck Bridge, oil on canvas by J W Carmichael c1840. This to the east of the Wetheral bridge and has, in the centre, the Corby Lion (inse

Tullie House Museum & Art Gallery

Carlisle Library

Mr Pry descended to examine the quarry beside the bridge in 1832 and this was still open when J W Carmichael visited in 1835 to make this sketch.

The inset shows the crane for lifting stones which was behind Edenside and later used for the bowling green (see page 82).

Tullie House Museum & Art Gallery

railroad is to cross the River Eden," so the site had been established. "On Thursday, 25 March 1830," *The Citizen* reported, "the foundation stone of Corby Bridge was laid near Wetheral, being the commencement of that great undertaking, the Railway between Newcastle and Carlisle." This was performed by Henry Howard amongst large crowds, with flags flying, bands playing and much ale consumed. The *Journal* said in September 1830, "the building of the bridge over the Eden at Wetheral, the Corby Beck bridge, the culverts and the whole of the mason work between Corby and Carlisle have been let to Messrs Robson & Co. of Newcastle." The newspaper added that the, "contracts can be put an end to at any time by the engineers if they fail in any part of their undertaking," which is appropriate as Robson was sacked part way through and his place taken by the Carlisle contractors Nixson & Denton.

On 18 May 1831 Henry Howard's son, Philip Henry Howard, had the honour of laying the first stone for Corby Beck Bridge, this being from designs by George Larmer and not as large as the one at Wetheral. Only a few hundred yards separated the two bridges. A visit to the works was made by 'Mr Pry' in October 1832 and this appeared in *The Citizen*, "I resolved to walk along the cutting of the railway to see this much talked of Wetheral Bridge (I being a subscriber). I followed the line as well as I could and got at last to Wetheral where the machine lowers and raises the stones to the 'erection' as one of the workmen named it." Mr Pry descended to examine the quarry just beside the bridge and nearby he found, "four or five men above the knees in water clearing away the millrace wall which the flood of a few days before had brought down." He was able to cross by the scaffolding, "to see the Corby Bridge, which with the Wetheral Bridge reflects great credit on the contractor." But he considered, "the Corby [Beck] Bridge a silly waste of money."
There were many accidents in construction but Thomas Blackwell was very lucky. In May 1833 he fell 73 feet when a rope broke, landing him in the river. He was able to walk out of the water, "without assistance and resumed his employment on the following morning," stated the *Journal*.
The last stone on the Corby Beck Bridge was set on 16 October 1833 but work was far from completed, the newspapers reporting that on 31 March 1835 contractors were to, "try an experiment for supplying the night workers near Wetheral with light." All was finished to allow for opening as far as Greenhead on 19 July 1836 and to Newcastle in 1838.

Wetheral Station

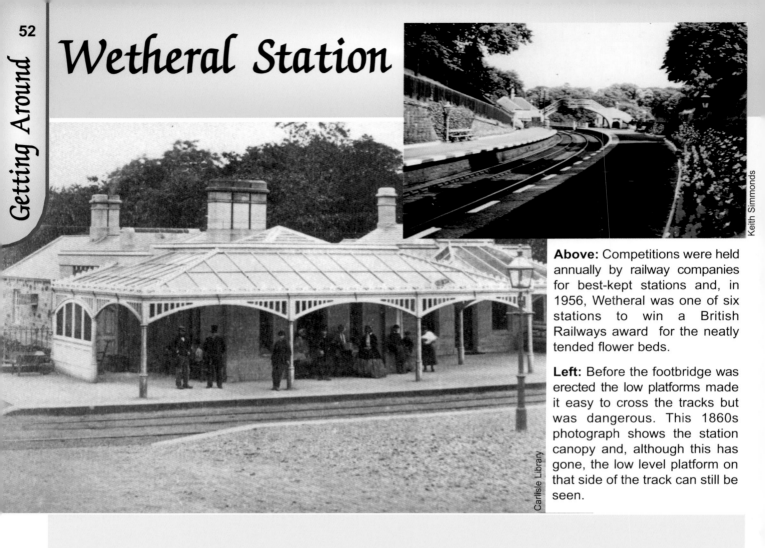

Keith Simmonds

Carlisle Library

Above: Competitions were held annually by railway companies for best-kept stations and, in 1956, Wetheral was one of six stations to win a British Railways award for the neatly tended flower beds.

Left: Before the footbridge was erected the low platforms made it easy to cross the tracks but was dangerous. This 1860s photograph shows the station canopy and, although this has gone, the low level platform on that side of the track can still be seen.

In 1872 an itinerant violinist, well-known in Carlisle, was seriously injured at Wetheral Station. Having taken his ticket at the booking office on the east-bound platform, John Harkness was crossing the line for the Carlisle train when the 4.15 pm from Newcastle came up. The *Carlisle Express* reported, "The poor man, who walks with a crutch, was not able to step upon the platform quickly enough and was stuck by the buffer of the engine in the side." This resulted, "in his fiddle being smashed to pieces and himself thrown onto the platform with several ribs broken."

Nothing was done at the time to remedy the danger, but things came to a head in January 1885 because of, "the exertions of Mr H Whitten of Edenwood House, Wetheral, who for some time past has been publishing a series of lively strictures on the general management of the Newcastle and Carlisle line and exposing the extremely dangerous character of the arrangements at Wetheral Station in particular," said the *Journal*. He took issue with, "the dangerous level crossing between two curves and the insufficiency of the platforms to accommodate with safety the crowds of excursionists who frequent Wetheral during the summer."

These complaints were brought to the notice of the Board of Trade who ordered the engineers of the North Eastern Company to remedy some of the defects. As a result, "an extensive scheme of improvements is now under consideration," reported the newspaper. On 26 January 1885 the Board of Trade Inspector, Major-General Hutchinson, accompanied by Mr Tennant, the general manager of the NER, with six others, "paid a visit to Wetheral Station for the purpose of enquiring into the complaints," said the *Journal*. After pacing the platform numerous times and examining the curves, the Major-General "made several notes and departed for Carlisle at two o'clock." The *Journal* added, "Many people who were upon the platform during the visit watched the proceedings with much interest, the appearance of so many high officials being taken as evidence that something was at last about to be done." There was no delay in the Board of Trade report which was published in full a month later in the *Journal*. Observations were made and measurements given, the conclusions being:

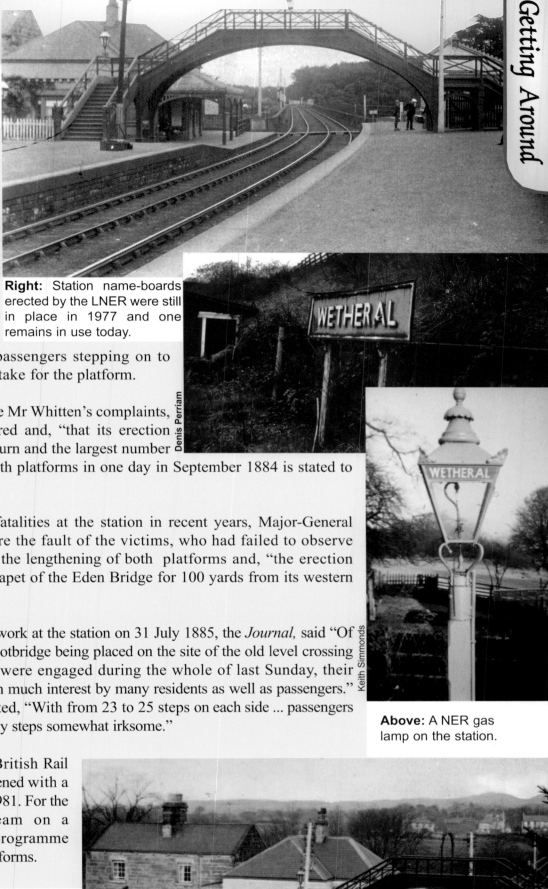

Right: The footbridge of 1885, seen here when new, is the one in use today.

1. That the level crossing at the station is a most dangerous one.

2. That the platform on the south side (for Carlisle) is inadequate both in length and in width.

Right: Station name-boards erected by the LNER were still in place in 1977 and one remains in use today.

3. That the bridge over the Eden which adjoins, is a source of danger and of passengers stepping on to and over the parapet in mistake for the platform.

It was pointed out that, before Mr Whitten's complaints, a footbridge had been ordered and, "that its erection would be commenced in its turn and the largest number of passengers alighting at both platforms in one day in September 1884 is stated to have been 384."

While there had been two fatalities at the station in recent years, Major-General Hutchinson found these were the fault of the victims, who had failed to observe bye-laws. He recommended the lengthening of both platforms and, "the erection of a railing on the south parapet of the Eden Bridge for 100 yards from its western end."

Reporting on the progress of work at the station on 31 July 1885, the *Journal,* said "Of the massive and costly iron footbridge being placed on the site of the old level crossing ... the company's workmen were engaged during the whole of last Sunday, their operations being watched with much interest by many residents as well as passengers." But the newspaper commented, "With from 23 to 25 steps on each side ... passengers may find the ascent of so many steps somewhat irksome."

Above: A NER gas lamp on the station.

The station was closed by British Rail in January 1967 but was re-opened with a special train on 5 October 1981. For the re-opening a job-creation team on a youth opportunities programme cleaned up the neglected platforms.

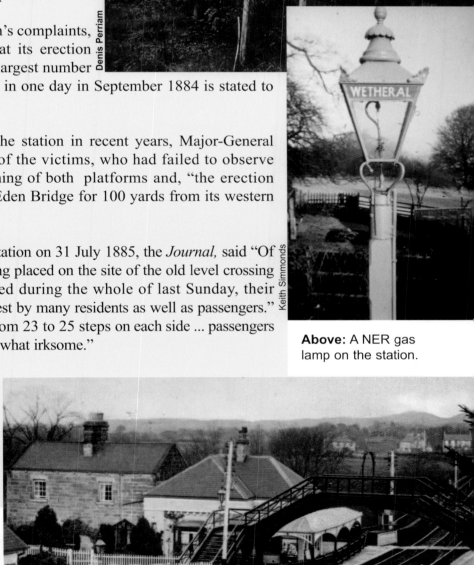

Right: This postcard was posted in 1910 and by that date safety fences had been erected and the stationmaster's house increased to two storeys.

Tolls

When Corby Bridge was first built there was no pedestrian walkway as the bridge was constructed purely to carry the railway across the river. However, to walk along the railway track was a convenient (if rather dangerous) way of crossing the river between the two villages, and it saved a ferry fare.

Trespass on the railway became such a problem that steps had to be taken to stop it. People risked their lives crossing the river by the bridge along the railway track. "Yielding to incessant demand the railway authorities conceded to a footway," said the *Journal*. It was decided to offer an alternative at a small charge by building a footway on the north face of the bridge and charging a toll. A cast iron plaque on the ironwork of the footway records the date as 1851 and the names of the engineer and contractor. To ensure that tolls were collected there was a small window with a cash slot at Wetheral Station and at Corby level crossing a wooden toll-collector's box was built onto the house for the keeper.

The success of the scheme was the subject of a memorial to the directors of the N & C R in 1853 (*Journal* 26 February). For those passengers living on the Corby side it cost an extra $1/_2$d to catch a train at Wetheral Station using the toll bridge and in 1891, "the residents on the Corby side got up agitation for the abolition of the toll,"stated the *Journal*. There were continued petitions to the railway company for the tolls to cease, this being described in 1911 as a, "great grievance in the district." Only on a Sunday were those on the way to church at Wetheral allowed free passage. The rules for Sunday passage were displayed on a notice at the Wetheral end of the bridge (see top of the next page).

James Steel of Eden Bank had acted as an intermediary and in 1896 the NER agreed they would free the toll if the Parish Council would pay £100 per annum (which they said was less than that normally collected). But in 1913 the Parish Council said that as the bridge, "did not connect with a public road they could not take any action to abolish the toll" (*Journal* 25 July 1913).

Left: Toll keepers cottage on the Corby side. The woo
toll booth fascia (see bottom right of next page) has
gone.

Below: Toll booth at Station House on the Wetheral si
the viaduct.

Cast into the footbridge are the names of the engineer and contractor.

On the Wetheral side the toll was collected by the stationmaster, but at the Corby box a special employee was required.

In 1911 a columnist in the *Journal* looked back thirty five years with recollections of Wetheral. He said there were John Armstrong and 'Willie' Tiffin who lived as neighbours in two houses, formerly the old workhouse. Armstrong afterwards had charge of the bridge at the Corby side and took the tickets from the foot passengers. John was always ready for a crack and had a large fund of anecdotes and history of the district. In January 1909 the *Journal* reported the retirement of the Armstrongs from the, "Bridge Toll Box, Corby Crossing, [on the] last day of 1908, the departure from the above of the Misses Armstrongs, who with their father (John) and mother and grandfather before them, have occupied the house and served the NER for 50 years." The girls were presented with umbrellas and were to start a guest house in Corby.

In 1955 the argument about the toll reached the national press. The *Daily Mail,* no less, reported, "They call it the 'twopenny village'. An extra 2d. is added to every train ticket, to every bus ride, to every bill paid in shops across the river, and even to a call at the doctor's.
THE PLACE is the tiny village of Great Corby, Cumberland.
THE REASON for the nickname? Villagers have to pay a penny toll every time they cross a footbridge to reach-and leave-the railway station."

The article went on to explain that the villagers contended that the British Transport Commission had no authority to levy the toll. Mr J B Pearson, a 72 year old retired engineer living in Wetheral had looked up the original Act of Parliament and found that it did not apply to the footbridge. "What did the Commission do about it? Painted out the the reference to the Act and still charged 1d."

Mrs Kirkpatrick wrote in 1956 that she witnessed the end; "the footbridge was subject to a toll of ½d each way and when British Railways raised it to a penny there was a loud outcry from both villages. Eventually, after a great deal of trouble, the efforts of the Parish Council (who agreed to pay for the lighting), aided by an old resident who did not live to see the achievement of his ambition, the toll was abolished and the bridge is free."

NOT MUCH LONGER THEY HOPE

Cumberland News 27 January 1956

Above: Great Corby schoolchildren and teacher paying their tolls to cross the viaduct shortly before they were abolished.

Left: The viaduct footbridge today.

Wetheral Ferry

Keith Simmonds

Before the railway linked Wetheral and Corby in the 1830s, there were other ways of crossing the River Eden to save a detour of three miles via Warwick Bridge. The *Journal* in January 1893 said, "For some hundreds of years there has been a ford for horses and carts over the river between the two villages."

A later *Journal* article commented, "None of the works consulted carries any reference to it, but traces exist down the river to the ancient ford ... there used to be a road on the Corby side down to the river with a hedge on each side." In 12th century documents relating to Wetheral Priory mention is made of "Munchwath", this being the Monks' Ford which Prescott thought, "identical with the ford still existing [in 1897] 350 yards below the railway bridge." When the Fish Inn closed in 1907 (see page 94), it was given the name "Ferry Hill House" and it seems this had always been the route to the ferry. There was a similar road at Corby, opposite, which led down to Ferry Cottage. The *Journal* said that cottage "was the base of operations" and the home of the ferryman. While there was nothing to give a date, the newspaper thought, "a ferry was in existence at this point before the Conquest."

Most crossed safely but tragedy struck on Easter Sunday 1792, something recalled by Henry Howard in 1835, "Richard Gaddes was rowing the overloaded ferry boat to Corby, when the river was very high and rapid." The attraction was the annual opening of Mr Howard's Corby Castle walks to the public and, as a result, there was more traffic than usual. Margaret Kirkpatrick states, "A foolish young man named Foster stood up and began to rock the boat to frighten the women." This caused near panic among the passengers, many of them screamed and shrieked. "At the noise," said Mrs Kirkpatrick, "people came running to the river from all directions." They pulled branches from trees and tried to wade out, "but the water was too deep and swift."

Joe Armstrong

Continuing the story, Henry Howard said even when the boat was sinking, "Gaddes rowed it with the utmost energy," and managed to, "come within reach of the shore when it entirely sank." Hero of the day was the ferryman for, "although he could not swim," said Henry Howard, "and was up to his shoulders in water, managed to

Left: A ferry boat with a full load crossing the river. The youths are soaking the wooden wheels of a cart in the river to ensure that they do not dry out too much, thus causing the steel rims to loosen and come away from the wheel.

throw one passenger to the other, so that clinging together they were reached from the shore by George Hodgson of Corby and others." Twenty were rescued but, "two young men, who were going abroad, one of them from Wreay, were lost," said Mr Howard. Another passenger was carried away. Mrs Kirkpatrick said, "A little girl who floated downstream about 50 yards or so was got out in an exhausted condition." Recording the death of Richard Gaddes, aged 84, in February 1835, the *Journal* said, "It is remarkable that the person who imprudently swayed the boat was buried on the same day."

Ferry Cottage at the Corby side

This was not the only loss of life there. The *Pacquet* reported on the inquest in November 1834 on, "Margaret Milburn who kept the ferry boat over the River Eden at Wetheral." Margaret Milburn had come to public notice in 1827 when a painting by T C Hofland was exhibited at Carlisle. A reviewer talked, "of that good old lady who has plied at the ferry for 50 years and more ... the boat does not constitute the ferry without her masculine arms." Margaret had passed with a passenger at night and, in the darkness, had slipped, falling into the river unnoticed. When found, "her clothes were fastened to the pin on one of the oars," and thus entangled had prevented escape resulting in her accidental death.

Competition soon came with the erection of the railway viaduct which offered an alternative footbridge alongside the track. "What was a whole-time job before the toll path over the railway was opened became an incidental task afterwards and boats plied only as demand arose," said the *Journal*. In the 60 or 70 years before closure, the newspaper could only name three part-time ferrymen: John Hall, Mr Styles and William McIntyre. A newspaper photograph of 1938 shows a full boat crossing at Easter, but wartime economy seems to be the reason for the demise. In March 1941 the *Journal* carried a front page headline:

"Eden Valley Ferry May Be Doomed."

The story continued, "If the only boat which remains on the Wetheral-Great Corby ferry across the Eden is not replaced, and her condition after a winter lie-up is such that she is unlikely to float again, there will be no alternative to crossing the river by the footway along the railway bridge next summer." One old resident remarked: "Maybe our ferry will be just something of note in the books like all the other things that are gone past." But there was a sign of optimism. The newspaper said: "Local folk are slow to believe that so notable a feature of the district will disappear." Any possibility of revival came to an end when the toll on the bridge was abolished in 1955, but the ferry still operated on demand for many years after.

Left: Riders with their bicycles crossing the Eden by ferry on 12 July 1963.

Wetheral Buses

Right: A J Fidler's Albion at the Wetheral Green terminus early in the 1930s.

David Grisenthwaite

Below: A Ribble bus at Wetheral in 1984, about to leave for Lowry Hill.

David Grisenthwaite

Those wanting to get to Carlisle in the 19th century either walked, or if they could afford it, caught a train.

It was not until 2 July 1921 that Richard Percival of Carlisle introduced a bus service to Wetheral. He started a service from Brampton to Carlisle via Warwick Bridge, Wetheral and Cumwhinton, but in less than a year the diversion via Wetheral was abandoned, as there was sufficient traffic on the direct route and the railway service between Wetheral and Carlisle was more than adequate. However, he did operate excursions to Wetheral on a regular basis on Sundays at 6d (2.5p) each way. These continued throughout the 1920s with other proprietors joining in this lucrative trade.

Next was J J Wallis from 4 August 1923. He used three Albion buses to run an hourly service and from 21 April 1924 every half hour and on Sundays. He died in 1925 and his widow continued running the successful company. Then in June 1928 Alfred Fidler started a service from Market Street, Carlisle to Wetheral against Wallis, using a second hand 25-seater Leyland Lioness SM 5944. Mrs Wallis soon found the stress of competition too much and sold to Emmerson & Co in 1929 (who were owned by the railway).

J J Wallis' bus on the Wetheral service heading down Warwick Road in the mid - 1920s.

Denis Perriam

Right: Fidler's Leyland Lioness negotiates the 1928 floods in Warwick Road.

From 1931 United also ran in opposition to Wetheral (having taken over Emmersons) until they acquired Fidlers in 1934. United then had a monopoly and continued until their services at Carlisle were transferred to Ribble on 5 January 1969.

No changes were made when Cumberland Motor Services took over on 22 February 1986, but this was short-lived because Stagecoach Holdings Ltd purchased the company on 23 July 1987 and only the livery differed.

In providing the information above David Grisenthwaite ended by saying that on the present bus, "patronage is limited, but at least a link with the past survives."

Above: Tommy Bunyan and Mr Armstrong with a Wallis Albion on the Scotby, Wetheral run, parked at the terminus in Carlisle city centre (Crown and Mitre in the background).

Left: Fidler's Leyland Lioness bus in 1928. Seen here on a hot day, parked opposite Fantails with the radiator cover removed to cool the engine.

Left to right are Billy Ferguson (driver), Jack McNeil (Wetheral gillie), Ron Brunskill and Bob Brunskill.

Mary Ferguson (all images)

Corby Crossing

Ashley Kendall

Left: The level crossing today with the automatic barriers and signal box.

Below: From the air it is much easier to see the terrace of railway houses and the adjoining keeper's cottage opposite the signal box. The open area of the approach to the coal yard can be seen and the Corby Bridge Inn on the right.

Peter Armstong

When the railway opened there were manual gates which were operated by a keeper who lived on site and pushed the gates back and forth.

Coal drops were situated near the Corby Bridge Inn and the sandstone walls of the cells can still be seen there. The drops were abandoned in favour of a coal yard beyond the signal box and this remained in use after the withdrawal of steam in 1968.

A signal box replaced the previous arrangement in the late nineteenth century, the gates being opened and closed by means of a manual wheel from the box. Now electrically operated gates can be controlled by the signalman or by an approaching train.

Below left: A preserved Sir Nigel Gresley pulls a special over the crossing. The keeper's cottage is on the left and signal box on the right. A loaded coal lorry stands in the yard.

Below: Few photographs show the coal yard, but this view of Sir Nigel Gresley returning, conveniently shows it in the foreground.

Mimi & John Brown

Mrs Bull

NER Cottage Homes

Right: NER Cottage Homes at Great Corby opened by Viscount Grey (seventh from the left). Dr J G McBride, President of the Fund, is eleventh from the left.

A History of North Eastern Railway Architecture - Volume 3 (2005) gives details about the North Eastern Railway (NER) Cottage Homes and Benefit Fund.

Above: Ethel and Tommy Ramshaw outside No.8 Cottage Homes, July 1981.

"Its origins lie in the NER Employees War Relief Fund, which raised approximately £34,000 to support the families of NER men away at the war. The men then considered how a benefit scheme might be set up afterwards and in 1919 the company agreed to match their contributions over a period of three years, up to a limit of £20,000, and to provide ten shillings for every pound raised after that period ... The fund was formally established by an indenture of 18 February 1921 ... It was run by a committee of railwaymen, elected by the contributors ... Architectural and other professional services were provided gratis by the company, which also made land available at cost price ... Cottage homes were built in small groups throughout the former NER system and 181 had been completed by the end of 1927."

In the early days two sizes of homes were built, three bedroom and two bedroom, designed for employees incapacitated in the war, widows and families of employees killed during the war and employees compelled to retire through ill health. These were too large and expensive for some employees such as retired porters and platelayers so, in 1925, the first groups of one-storey, one bedroom cottages were opened.

The eight cottages at Great Corby, opened on 17 July 1925 by Viscount Grey, are of this type.

In 1972 the demand for these cottages from rail employees had reduced and so the Fund Committee decided to sell four of the cottages by auction at the Crown and Mitre Hotel at Carlisle. Incidentally one of these, No.8, was purchased by a retiring railway worker, Thomas Ramshaw, who wished to move to the area from Hull with his wife, Ethel, in order to be closer to family in Carlisle, namely one of the authors of this book.

Below and above: The cottage homes at Corby are set out in a semi-circle facing onto each other, thus promoting a neighbourly atmosphere for the residents.

Great Corby Village Hall

Philanthropist Henry Howard left two £100 shares in the Newcastle & Carlisle Railway in 1842, "for the purpose of establishing a Reading Room or Institution for the literary improvement of the young men of Great and Little Corby." Fund raising soirées were held but it was not until 1877 that this was built at a cost of £400. To commemorate Queen Victoria's Diamond Jubilee in 1897, a caretaker's house was added, costing £350, all raised by public subscription. This then formed the basis of the village hall and ever since has been the centre of social activities for more than a century. Groups and societies, such as the Women's Institute, have met there over the years. It has been the venue for table top sales, local drama performances, variety shows etc..

The Great Corby Drama Club ran in the village from 1994 - 1998 on Saturday mornings. It was organised by Jos Curtis until her increasing work commitments intervened. The 12 dancing Princesses in 1995 was based on a Brothers Grimm Fairy Tale

Above: Laying the foundation stone for the village hall extensions (caretaker's house) of 1897. The onlookers stand on the road facing the front of the new building.

Inset: Mrs Hills, of Corby Castle, laid the stone on 30 Dec 1897, The building was named Jubilee Cottage.

Right: The village hall today.

Below left: A table top sale in the village hall about 1982. Olive Arnold, Edie Downey and Ethel Ramshaw are being served by Martin Armstrong, Nicola Prudham, Helen Holmes and Andrew Holmes.

Below right: Madge Cowan cuts the cake at the Women's Institute 70th anniversary.
Back row from the left: Susan Bull, Isobel Watson, Joyce Gorst, Helen Invest, Alison Watt, Doreen Mills, Betty Steele, Pat Johnson, Kate Taprill, Susan Holmes.
Front row: Peggy Little, Lillian Kendrick, Hilda Coulthard, Peggy Cowan, Madge Cowan, Shirley Powell, Kathleen Davidson, Margaret Wareing, Mary Lumsden. Seated are Ethel Ramshaw, Audrie Lowrie and Nora Suart.

Cumberland News, both images

Events in the hall

about 12 princesses who leave their castle at night against their father's wishes, and go off in boats to dance and to meet princes in an underground castle.
Between 1999 and 2006 four variety shows were staged in the village hall. These pictures are from the 1999 production which featured, amongst other acts, a collection of male ballet dancers.

Right: The programme for 'Two Brothers', a 1994 production of the Great Corby Drama Society.

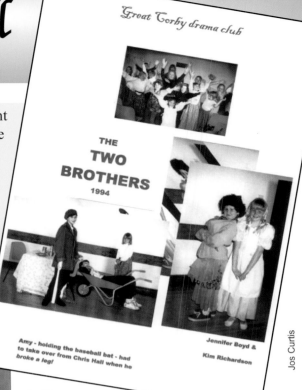

Great Corby drama club

THE
**TWO
BROTHERS**
1994

Amy - holding the baseball bat - had to take over from Chris Hall when he broke a leg!

Jennifer Boyd & Kim Richardson

Jos Curtis

Left:
'Abba' performing in the 1999 variety show.

Below left: Climax of the ballet!.

Below: The trio of David Summers, Karl and Joanne in the 1999 variety show.

Bottom left: The Finale.

Bottom right: Two little fairies.

Joe Armstrong all images

The Home Front

Ashley Kendall

Keith Simmonds

Top: Wounded soldiers from local military war hospitals were entertained at Wetheral Bowling Club in 1915.
Above: A concerned father brings his two sons to Mr Farrer to have their photos taken before going off to war.
Right: Recruitment posters at first played on the sympathies that Britons had for the treatment of Belgium in 1914.

Margaret Kirkpatrick said "this lovely peaceful village, dreaming beside its river in the August sunshine of 1914 seemed very far removed from the horror of war."

At a parish council meeting in September 1915 it was said of the railway bridges at Wetheral and Corby, "at the beginning of the war these bridges were guarded by the military but the soldiers were subsequently withdrawn." Other than this, the first indication of war was the arrival of Belgian refugees at Merlewood, on the Plains Road, with tales of atrocities. These were not the only refugees to come to the area, aliens being banished from anywhere within a radius of military facilities.

Thus many people from the North East, close to the River Tyne and naval yards, had to leave. Three German families came to live in Wetheral and Great Corby. One villager complained, "before the Germans entered Wetheral he could see the board - Your King and Country Wants You. One Hundred Thousand Men Wanted. Come and Join Us - but since ... that board had gone."

Some of the men, although of German origin, were naturalised, but this did not stop a petition being submitted by locals for their removal.

Denis Perriam

REMEMBER BELGIUM

ENLIST TO-DAY

And On Active Service

Chairman of the 'Stop the War Committee' in London was solicitor James Scott Duckers who had been brought up in Wetheral and was articled in Carlisle. As a conscientious objector he refused to fight and spent four years in gaol, writing a book on his experiences. Margaret Duckers, sister of James, became a nurse and was one who did not return from Salonica. Margaret Kirkpatrick said, "one by one the village lads went off ... and long familiar names appeared on the casualty lists." Prisoners of war in Germany benefitted from socks knitted under the guidance of Miss Creighton of Eden Mount, who was the honorary secretary of the Carlisle Womens' League. These were sent to Kut Camp where some soldiers escaped and the newspapers said, "the men made their way out of captivity wearing on their feet the excellent socks made at Wetheral."

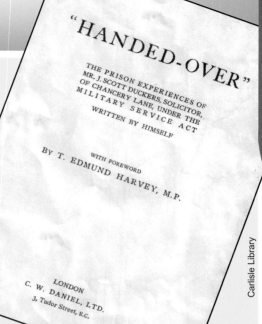

"HANDED-OVER"

THE PRISON EXPERIENCES OF MR. J. SCOTT DUCKERS, SOLICITOR, OF CHANCERY LANE, UNDER THE MILITARY SERVICE ACT
WRITTEN BY HIMSELF

WITH FOREWORD
BY T. EDMUND HARVEY, M.P.

LONDON
C. W. DANIEL, LTD.
3, Tudor Street, E.C.

Carlisle Library

Lcᵉˡ JOHN LEONARD CATON	BORDER	6 SEPT 1915	FRANCE	Lt. PERCY LANGHORN THOMPSON	D.L.I.	12 JUNE 1917	BELGIUM
C.S.M. THOMAS WOOD		4 " 1916	"	Rᶠˡᵉ ARTHUR HILL	K.Rᶠˡᵉ	31 JULY "	FRANCE
Ptᵉ STANLEY STEEL	R.FUS.	14 OCT "	"	Ptᵉ GILBERT STEEL CLARKE	W.C.Yᵒ	28 OCT "	BELGIUM
" THOMAS BELL	W.C.Yᵒ	26 APL. 1917	"	" J.W. BEDWELL SLATER	W.YORKS	26 DEC "	"

Ptᵉ ROBERT WATSON	E.YORKS	27 MAY 1918	FRANCE	Ptᵉ WILLIAM GEO. BARNFATHER	BORDER	4 NOV 1918	FRANCE
" THOMAS TAYLOR M.M.	Nᵈᵉᵈ Dᵗ	8 OCT "	BELGIUM	" JAMES PARK	R.C.A	12 " "	"
Sᵉʳ GEORGE BOWMAN	R.E.	18 " "	SALONICA	Sᵗ Nᵘʳˢᵉ MARGARET E. DUCKERS	Q.A.I.M.N.S.R.	16 MAY "	SALONICA

Below and Above: The war memorial was dedicated on 10 July 1921 this being from a design by J H Martindale and the oakwork carved by Thomas Lawson. It took the form of a lychgate for the church and Canon Loftie said, "It will be a lasting reminder of those who fell for their country, for carved in raised letters upon oaken panels there is a complete list of the names of all those commemorated by the memorial."

ROLL OF HONOUR

1914 1918

GREAT CORBY

THESE SERVED THEIR COUNTRY DURING THE GREAT WAR THREE MAKING THE SUPREME SACRIFICE

Capt. J.R.L.THOMPSON M.C. Lieut. J. BEAVAN
Lieut. P. THOMPSON Lieut. W.W. ROUTLEDGE
Sergt. J. BURROWS M.M. Sergt. G. COLLINS
Corpl A. BURROWS Corpl T. NEVILLE
Corpl J. R. BOUTLEDGE
Sapper G. BOWMAN Private J. HIND
Private J. BOWMAN Air Mec. J. HOPKINS
" T. BOWMAN Gunner P. HOPKINS
" R. BOWMAN Private J. KINCHIN
" T. BANKS " F. KINCHIN
Air Mec. J. BARKER Gdsmn R. LAMB
Private J. BROWN Private T. MCDONALD
" A. BROATCH Sapper T. NOBLE
" J. BROATCH Private E. SIMPSON
" T. BURROWS " J. SIMPSON
" J. BURNETT " A. SMITH
" E. BELL " B. SMITH
" E. DOBSON " L. SOULSBY
" T. FORRESTER Seaman H. SOWERBY
" R. FORRESTER Sapper T. TAYLOR M.M.
" W.E. GRIMLEY Private W.C. TYRREL
Stoker W. HARTLEY Sapper T. E. WILTON
Sapper G. HIND Air Mec. W. WEBSTER

KILLED IN ACTION
THEIR NAME LIVETH FOR EVERMORE

Above: The war memorial at Great Corby is a plaque on the front wall of the village hall.

Carlisle Library

MEMORIAL GATE, WETHERAL CHURCH

Peace

At the end of the war with, "the church bell joyfully pealing the good news ... distinctly heard in Cumwhitton," Mrs Kirkpatrick said, "nothing was ever the same again."

With the coming of peace local communities throughout the country arranged celebrations and Wetheral was no exception. The Peace Committee invited all the inhabitants of Wetheral, Wetheral Pasture and Wetheral Shields to tea on the village green.

Children were asked to meet at the school at 2.00 pm to receive medals and march down to the Green. Prizes were offered for the best display of wild flowers on staves to be carried in the procession, one for boys, one for girls and one for boys and girls under 10.

A full programme of sports was arranged as set out on the poster below.

Keith Simmonds

PEACE
CELEBRATIONS AT WETHERAL
ON JULY 19TH, 1919.

The Committee invites all the inhabitants of WETHERAL, WETHERAL PASTURE, and WETHERAL SHIELDS to TEA on the VILLAGE GREEN, on Saturday, 19th July, 1919.
CHILDREN meet at the SCHOOL at 2 p.m. to receive MEDALS and march down to Green.
PRIZES will be given for the Best Display of WILD FLOWERS fixed on Staves, to be carried in the Procession, one for Boys and Girls under 14 years, and one for Boys and Girls under 10 years.
SPORTS at 3. TEA for CHILDREN at 4. TEA for ADULTS from 5.

PROGRAMME OF SPORTS
(CONFINED TO THE TOWNSHIP OF WETHERAL)
To commence at 3·0 p.m.

1. FLAT RACE for Boys under 8.
2. FLAT RACE for Girls under 8.
3. THREE-LEGGED RACE for Boys under 11.
4. EGG and SPOON RACE for Girls under 14.
5. FLAT RACE for Boys under 14 (twice round the Green).
6. FLAT RACE for Girls under 11.
7. NEEDLE AND THREAD RACE.
8. FLAT RACE for Boys under 11.
9. FLAT RACE for Girls under 14.
10. WHEELBARROW RACE for Boys under 14.
11. STONE and BASKET RACE for Girls and Boys under 14.
12. FLAT RACE, Open. About 120 yards.
13. SKIPPING RACE for Girls under 14.
14. SACK RACE for Boys under 14.
15. PILLOW FIGHT.
16. BUN WORRY.
17. THREE-LEGGED RACE (Open).
18. TUG-OF-WAR.
19. WRESTLING for Boys under 14.
20. LADIES' EGG and SPOON RACE.

No Competitor to take more than ONE FIRST, or Two Prizes in all.

A BAND
Will be in attendance and PLAY for DANCING.
HALSTEAD & SONS, PRINTERS, CARLISLE.

Above: This photograph by Joseph Farrer shows his daughter Florence proudly displaying her bicycle which she had decorated especially for the peace celebrations described on the adjacent poster.

The *Cumberland News* 22 July 1919 reported "Peace medals were distributed to the children at the school before the procession started round the village." On this occasion J H Martindale, chairman of the Parish Council and the Rev Green, the vicar, "addressed some appropriate remarks to the young folks."

Subscriptions of £100 had been given for the celebrations and the newspaper stated, "any surplus left over after...would be given to the soldiers and sailors of the township."

Bobbie Leyland

The Phoney War

AEROPLANE CRASH NEAR CORBY

.A.F. CRASH AT CORBY

PILOT'S FORTUNATE ESCAPE

WITH wings brushing the tree tops, a Royal Air Force fighter aeroplane ...ared over Corby at noon on Tuesday and ...ashed into a field near Keeper's Cottage. The pilot, Pilot Officer G. Evans, ...aggered from the wrecked machine, ...aken but practically unhurt. He walked ...o the cottage, where facial cuts were ...eated by Mrs. Holmes.

It appears that the aeroplane was on a ...ight from Folkestone, Kent, to Usworth, ...urham, and running short of fuel, the ...ilot tried to make a forced landing, but ... descending his right wing touched a ...ee, tearing off the branches about forty ...eet from the ground. The 'plane nose-...ived and crashed in the field. Its engine ...as nearly torn away and one wing was ...attered—the pilot had a miraculous ...scape.

On Wednesday the wreckage was re-...oved by an R.A.F. squad, drawn from ...eighbouring aerodromes.

Carlisle Journal 6 January 1939

"We shall never stop, never weary, and never give in."
The Prime Minister.

Above & top right: Churchill's words printed on Wetheral postcards.

Left and Above: In the months leading up to the outbreak of war in 1939 there would be increased activity in the skies of Cumbria as desperately needed pilots were trained. This is illustrated by a crash near Great Corby in January 1939. This article and photograph from the *Journal* tells the story.

Above: The Wetheral platoon of the Home Guard, probably photographed outside the vicarage. Third form the left on the back row is Andrew Elliot, elder brother to Reg Elliot.

Left: The Welcome Home Fund Committee in 1940. No one knew when the war would end but these ladies were ready for any eventuality.
Back: Mrs G Lawson, Connie Hewgill, Mrs Sayer, Mrs McKiever, Toddles Lawson.
Middle: Milly Rowlands, Mrs Campling, Mrs Cowan,
Front: Mother? Mrs P Hopkins, Mrs Hutchinson.

RAF links

Above: Reg Elliot in later life, seen here in July 1992.

Right: Reg. Elliot is third from the left in this photo of the crew of their Lancaster bomber nicknamed "Never a Dull" followed by "Wizo Bish".

Reg Elliot

One young man from Great Corby who served in the RAF during World War 2 and survived to tell the tale was Reg Elliot, born and brought up in the village. The family moved from Scotland in 1903 when his father, John, took employment as a gamekeeper and gillie at Corby Castle. They lived at Pheasant Cottage where Reg was born in 1914. Most of the children had Scottish names but, according to Reg they had 'ran out of these' when he came along.

At the start of the war Reg volunteered for service in the RAF and trained as a navigator and bomb aimer on Lancasters. He served in 101 Squadron RAF Ludford Marine Bomber Command, based at Ledford Minor, a village in Lincolnshire.

Reg took part in thirty nine operations over enemy territory. Over 55,000 aircrew were killed during the war, serving with Bomber Command, of whom 7,000 have no known grave. This is the highest casualty rate of any force of similar size in the history of warfare and its members were, of course, volunteers. About half of the airmen in Reg Elliot's base were killed in the war, often aged only 19-22 years.

Above: One who did not return except to be buried in Wetheral cemetery.
Not far from this stone is the grave of Pilot Officer Harvey Strong Little who was killed in action on 31 May 1942 aged 31.

Right: Reg's family in front of Pheasant cottage before Reg and brother Charlie were born.
From left: Margaret (mother), Janet, John (father), Margaret (sister), Gilbert (Bert), Andrew, Isabel.

After his father's death in 1936 Reg's family moved to Raygarth, Great Corby, where Reg, who never married, lived the rest of his life. After the war he worked at 14 MU (RAF Maintenance Unit) at Kingstown, Carlisle, thus maintaining his links with the RAF, and in his spare time was active in village affairs for many years as a parish councillor.

Reg Elliot

Crash at Great Corby

The repaired chimney in Great Corby.

An inquest report on the incident above states, "On 31 January 1942 an aircraft took off from Silloth at 10.45 am on a local training flight. Over the village of Great Corby the plane was flying very low, so low that it struck a chimney used jointly by two houses, damaging same and also the roofs of the two houses. It then rose slightly and travelled a distance of approximately 500 yards when it struck a bank top and burst into flames, careering on for about another 150 yards. It came to rest in a field at Birkhill where it burnt out." The young pilot's name was Douglas McIntosh Burgess, son of Charles H Burgess of Port Credit, Ontario, Canada. He is buried in Causewayhead cemetery, Silloth. His observer Sgt John Ralph Vigors Bones was also killed in the crash.

The story behind this tragic accident relates to two families, one of which lived in the village at the time. It is told by Mary Burgess (nee Snowball) who now lives in Canada. "My mother and dad and I emigrated in 1930 after my dad lost his business (chartered accountant) in the 1929 crash, so we went to Canada where my dad became a Senior Assessor of Corporate Income Tax under the Canadian Federal Government based in Toronto. We eventually lived in Port Credit, west of Toronto and next door to the Burgess family. There were six boys and one girl. Tom, Doug and Anna all attended the local high school. The other boys were either in University or had graduated at this time. My dad became ill and died of cancer on 31 January 1937 (note this date - Doug's death and Mr C H Burgess birthday).

My Mother and I returned to England in May and went to Great Corby, to my grandparents. Mother subsequently remarried - to Mr T V Hutchinson of Glenholme, Gt Corby. When the war came five Burgess boys served overseas and all made our home their leave base. In the meantime Tom and I kept up a correspondence so were very glad to be able to see each other again and in 1946 we married. Tom was in Europe (Italy up to Holland) for two years, so we didn't see each other a great deal, but have lived a very happy life (we celebrated our 60th in 2006) ... We have two sons, five grandchildren and one great grandchild and another on the way. Tom was Professor of Animal Science at the University of Guelph ... At this point (January 2008) Tom is 87 and I am 86 in March, both in pretty good health ... What did I do during the war years? I attended The Gregg School in Carlisle taking the Civil Service exams and was sent to the High Court of Justice Probate Division and was based in Carlisle in Abbey St. (the office eventually moved) and did Red Cross nursing at the Infirmary in my spare hours."

Mary Burgess

Pilot Officer Burgess.

The inquest went on to report that, "the flight was authorised to carry out various exercises, landings, turns and single engine flying within ten miles of Silloth ... they had no business to be at Great Corby." It appears that in the 'exuberance of youth' Douglas decided to 'buzz' Mary's house with tragic consequences. She was not at home at the time, being at work.

Mary and husband Tom still come back to the UK every year and visit Great Corby. Several of the photographs in this book were kindly provided by her.

The Corby connection with the family was broken in 1950 when Mary's mother was widowed for the second time and went to live with them in Canada.
She passed away in 1989 at the age of 94.

Tom and Mary on a visit to Cumbria in May 2008.

Mary Burgess

Tom and Mary's wedding.

Women's Land Army

Bettie Baird

Vera Timperon (both images)

Left: Geltsdale (formerly Wandales, see page 48) on Plains Road seen here about 1944 when the mansion was used as a hostel for the girls in the Land Army.
Below: Land Girls at the entrance to Geltsdale. Back row (left to right): Ellen Ransome, Margaret, Sarah.
Front row: Alice Watson, Teresa Kelly, Vera Timperon, Sylvia Petlar.

The Women's Land Army was established during World War 1 as the Government needing to re-vitalise home agriculture, fearing food shortages. Extra labour was also needed as men were being called up for the armed forces. Volunteers were required again during World War 2 and by 1939, there were 39,000 women working on the land which increased to 75,000 by 1945. The girls of the Land Army looked after animals, ploughed the fields, dug up potatoes, harvested crops and killed rats. They dug and hoed for 48 hours a week in the winter and 50 hours a week in the summer. As there was not enough machinery to go round they often had to work with old fashioned equipment, such as horse-drawn hand ploughs, and to harvest crops by hand.

Bettie Baird

Above: Bettie Baird, centre, learning to set rat traps.
Below Left: Land Girls sitting on a potato clamp after harvesting the potatoes.

Frances Apps (nee Addison) came from Red House Farm, Great Orton and worked at various farms around the north until (in 1943) she was offered employment by Captain Thorpe of the WLA office in Carlisle. She was to be in charge of the Wetheral Land Army Hostel at Geltsdale (formerly RAF Wetheral) which housed 40 girls. The staff consisted of a cook and two elderly wardens and part of Frances' duties was to drive a large truck which took the girls to their farms and then collected them all again in the evening. In spite of the hard work they enjoyed various activities including local hoeing competitions for Cumberland and Westmorland.

One vivid memory was the night the girls were invited to Wetheral Village Hall to see a film made by the army about the liberating of the Belsen Concentration Camp. The film had been made specially to inform local people, who were often unaware of what was happening elsewhere, about the horrors being perpetrated by the Nazi regime. It was the most horrific sight they had ever seen. Frances was at Wetheral for about two years before she married Driver Jack Apps (see next page). She then moved to a farm in Ashford, Kent where her duties were mostly to do with milk rounds. Mr and Mrs Apps now live in retirement in Wakefield.

Vera Timperon

Muriel Hunter, Doris Nerdick, Belle Crawford, Vera Timperon, Nancy Cummins

Land Girls

In February 2008, as this book was being prepared, the Land Army was in the news when the Government announced that they had finally decided to recognise the work of the Land Girls by awarding a commemorative badge to the survivors.

Top Right: Frances Apps (nee Addison) receiving the prize for the Wetheral Hostel team after they had won the inter-county hoeing competition.
Right: The winning team.
Far Right: Frances in her WLA uniform.

Frances Apps (all three images)

Vera Timperon (nee White) of Scotby and Bettie Baird (nee McDonald) of Carlisle were interviewed by the *Cumberland News* and described their experiences. Vera said that the Geltsdale Hostel was luxury compared to their first farm accommodation, "The bedroom was freezing and we slept in all our clothes. They were religious and wouldn't even let us have our sweet coupons, but we had such a laugh. The first day they told us to feed the calves, which came running so we dropped the buckets and fled."

Bettie still has a crooked finger from getting it trapped in a potato sorting machine. She said "Picking potatoes is a back-breaking job. There were usually quite a few of us on this job. The man with the tractor and digger would drive down the drill leaving a layer of potatoes to be picked up. If you were quick you could have a little rest before the tractor came back." Towards the end of the war she trained as a rat-catcher and remembers having to pick up the poisoned animals to bury them in manure heaps.

John Walton

Vera Timperon/ Cumberland News

Above: Land Girls picking strawberries at Wetheral with Stan Walton, Market Gardener.
From the left are two land girls from the north east, Mr W E Walton, Mrs E Walton, Irene Graham (nee Dice) and Stan Walton.

Left: The wedding of Frances Addison to Driver Jack Apps at Wetheral Church on 4 August 1945. Frances recalls the names of some of the guard of honour.
On the left, Dorothy and to her right Vera Timperon. From the right, second in is Edna and third in is Evelyn Pearson. This wedding was after the war ended and the Land Army was not disbanded until 1949.

Horticulture

Ashley Kendall via Slee Family

Carlisle Library

Wetheral and District Horticultural Society.

Flower Show

POULTRY SHOW,

SPORTS, &c.

Thursday, September 3rd,

1914.

IN PRIZES **£50** IN PRIZES

Schedule of Prizes.

HALSTEAD AND SONS, PRINTERS, CASTLE STREET, CARLISLE.

Above: A programme for the Flower Show in 1914 which was cancelled due to the outbreak of war.

Above: Slee's stall in the Covered Market offered produce grown by them as market gardeners at Wetheral. Their nurseries were at Castle Grounds where the former workhouse had been.

The Wetheral and District Horticultural Society held an annual show in the early part of the 19th century. The show had prizes for home grown produce as well as a poultry show and a full range of sporting activities with attractive prizes for the winners. There was a cottagers class to encourage entries by local amateur gardeners. Prizes were sponsored by local gentlefolk and business owners. The range of activities at a typical show can be seen on the show poster opposite for 1912.

An interesting prize was that given by a local beekeeper for the best exhibit of honey. Beekeeping was a popular local industry in the past. In 1904 the Cumberland Bee Keeping Association recorded thirteen members in Wetheral and Great Corby District. John R Halls of Halls' Cottage, Great Corby being the local Honorary Secretary.

It was much later that the firm Judge's Honey came to Great Corby. Jeffrey Judge tells the story, "My great grandfather had kept bees and my father, a miner at Hallbankgate and who later worked at the brickworks, lived at Brampton and also kept bees. By the 1950s he had a lot of bees and decided to start his own business. He moved to Great Corby, producing and bottling honey in premises behind the Queen Inn. The business grew quickly, eventually employing sixteen people and, to maintain supply, much of the honey was imported from abroad. In 1986 the firm was supplying honey to the Co-op, Superdrug and Asda when it was bought out by Rowntrees, who continued at Corby until about 1990. Nestle then took over and transferred the business to another of their plants in Hatfield." That signalled the end of commercial honey production in Great Corby.

The Castle under gardener (right) was Mrs Jean Ruddick's brother-in-law. Although the garden in this picture looks fairly bare, the gardens were very well kept; they kept the big house supplied with fruit and vegetables, and the green houses were full of peaches and other fruits. Villagers could pick strawberries in season - though these would have to be weighed and paid for.

Jean Ruddick

Above: Making a beehive at Great Corby about 1940.

Jean Ruddick

Above: Corby Castle Estate gardeners (Gardener Caulfield and under gardener Reay).

WETHERAL & DISTRICT
HORTICULTURAL SOCIETY.
PRESIDENT   T. S. STRONG, ESQ.

THE ANNUAL FLOWER
SHOW
Poultry Show & Sports
WILL BE HELD NEAR

WETHERAL ABBEY
ON
THURSDAY, AUGUST 29TH, 1912,
to be opened by Mrs. BOLTON, The Wandales, Wetheral, at 2-30 p.m.,

WHEN UPWARDS OF **£50** WILL BE GIVEN IN PRIZES.

SILVER CUP, given by JAMES WATT, Esq., J.P., for Cottagers' Class.

WRESTLING
under Rules of the Cumberland & Westmorland Association.

"GARTH MARR" SOLID SILVER CHALLENGE CUP | SILVER WATCH given by the Cumberland & Westmorland Association
AND SUBSTANTIAL MONEY PRIZES | and MONEY PRIZES for Wrestling for Boys not over 16 Years of age.

Special Prize of 5/-, given by a Local Beekeeper, for the Best Exhibit of Honey.

SPORTS.

Prizes for 80 Yds. Handicap for Boys under 12 | 7/6 for PILLOW FIGHT
" 100 " " " 16 | 5/- for PEA GUESSING COMPETITION
" 100 " " Girls " 14 | £4 & Silver Cup, as above, for 10st. Wrestling
" Threading Needle Race for Girls 14 | £5 for 12st. WRESTLING
£1 for OLD PENNY PITCHING | 10/- and Silver Watch for Wrestling for Boys not over 16 Years
10/- for OBSTACLE RACE | £1 for Weight Guessing (Block Test) Competition
10/- for CUP SMASHING | and Prizes for Tug-of-War, Dancing, &c.
1/6 for TOBY |

The Chadwick Memorial Band
will be in attendance and play for Dancing until 9 p.m. Numerous other attractions.
REFRESHMENTS TO BE HAD ON THE GROUND AT REASONABLE CHARGES.
ADMISSION: 1 to 5 o'clock, 1/-; after 5 o'clock 6d.
Trains leave Carlisle at 1-50, 3-50, 5, and 6 p.m.   Return 3-26, 4-58, 6-3, 7-8 8-17, and 9-34 p.m.

HALSTEAD & SONS, PRINTERS, CASTLE STREET, CARLISLE.

Butchers in Corby

At the beginning of the 20th century R C Hetherington, known as Charlie Hetherington, ran his butcher business from Holly House, Great Corby, with his wife Hannah. In 1916 they moved the business to Howard House at the top of the bank. Charles Armstrong, grandson of Charlie, recalls being told that his grandfather delivered meat throughout the area with his horse-drawn van, as far as Hornsby Gate and, in those hard times, he never let anyone go without meat even if they could not pay. When Charlie died in 1928 Hannah and daughter, Madge, took over the business with Gordon Flitcroft, Billie Beattie and later Dick Little, working for them. Gordon Flitcroft is distinguished in that he was in the Canadian Army in World War 1 and was awarded the Victoria Cross.

In 1932 Madge married auctioneer Bob Armstrong, but continued to manage the business from Howard House.

About this time Dick Little left and set up his own butcher business, D & E Little, with his brother Teddy, across the road at Manor House.

Above: Mrs Hetherington outside Howard House which displays the family butcher sign.

Left: Old Holly House (before being renovated).

Inset: Inside the building can be seen sides of meat hanging.

Right: R C Hetherington at Holly House with his horse and covered cart for meat deliveries.

Charles Armstrong, all images

Right: Dick Little (right rear) and Freddie Steel (left) butchering a pig at the back of Manor House.

For many years the two businesses survived in competition with each other. Then after the war Hetheringtons was taken over first by Roddicks of Galashiels and later by McInnes of Armathwaite. Then, in the early 1950s Teddy Little bought the business and continued there until about 1958, when he died suddenly at work. That was the end of butchering at Howard House, but the business across the road continued. When Dick Little died Freddy Steele took over at Manor House to be followed by Ian Fyfe, who still lives at Corby Hill. The business finally closed in the early 1960s.

Above: Manor House many years ago.

Below Left: Group at the back of Manor House, Teddy Little, Thomas Wilson, Freddy Steele, Dick Little, Tommy HInd and Joe Wren.

Below: Charle's Armstrong's grandfather outside the Queen Inn with his horse-drawn meat delivery van.

Above: Madge Hetherington with the Chevrolet delivery van about 1932. They had several Chevrolet's over the years.

Corby School

Dorothy Carruthers

Above: Draft newspaper advert dated 18 December 1861; "Wanted at the beginning of 1862 - A master capable of imparting a good English Education. The endowment is at present £27 with a good house and garden and quarter pence.
Applications with Testimonials to be sent, post paid, to the Trustees of Great Corby School."

Above: Headmaster Dan Thompson with a group of pupils in the 1890s when girls were taught separately from boys. Mr Thompson was known for being 'good with a stick'.

A school at Great Corby was established in 1720 with an endowment of 25 acres of land, the rental of which provided part of the annual funding, the remainder coming from a quarterly charge to those attending. In 1794 Hutchinson stated the lands, "were of £6 or £7 rent - the scholars pay 2 shillings per quarter." This, in what amounted to a re-foundation of the school, was guaranteed by 50 trustees in 1790.

Under the terms of Henry Howard's will the school received, in 1842, the income of the interest of two £100 shares in the Newcastle & Carlisle Railway which paid 5% per annum. This, together with the land, brought in an income of £38 in 1847. With a more secure future the school and master's house were re-built by 1845 to which were added, in 1882, extensions costing £700. Under various Acts the school had become the responsibility of the Wetheral School Board and any fees were abolished. There was an average attendance of 80 pupils in 1901 which has now fallen to 50, still a healthy number for a village school.

Reg Elliot

Left: Playground exercises at the school in 1918.

Below: Advert for the new school dated August 1881.

TO BUILDERS.
TENDERS are invited for the ERECTION of a NEW SCHOOL at CORBY for the Wetheral School Board. Plans and Specifications may be seen and Quantities obtained until WEDNESDAY, the 24th, on which day Tenders must be delivered at my Office.
The Board do not bind themselves to accept the lowest or any Tender.
JAMES MURCHIE, Architect.
Devonshire Street.

Peter Moore

Right: A postcard, around 1900, showing Great Corby children outside Brook Villa (the school house).

Above: In country and some city schools children were encouraged to engage in pursuits which it was felt would help their future employment.

Here, early in the 20th century, boys under the supervision of Mr Beaton tend the Great Corby school garden.

Top left: A school warning sign, still to be seen on Sandy Lane.

Above: Great Corby school pupils in 1959. There are 67 on the photograph.

Right: Great Corby School in more recent times when Mrs Smith was headteacher.
The backdrop is the school, which from its architectural features shows its antiquity.

Water

On 17 June 1895 Wetheral and Great Corby received their first mains water. Before turning on the supply, Mr Steel, as chairman of the parish council, said that when the Newcastle and Carlisle Railway was built, "Cowran Cut was originally intended to be a tunnel, but in proceeding with the excavations the railway contractors found that the bank was so full of water that they were unable to get proper foundations for the masonry and they were therefore obliged to make it a cutting. The water which flowed from the cutting was collected in a conduit and carried down under the railway to Hard Bank."

In the scheme a holding tank was required and, "the railway company agreed to bring the water from Heads Nook to Wetheral in a six inch pipe under condition that the district council paid them an annual rental of £80." Costs were to be £1200 but it fell short of that amount.

Celebrations were held at Great Corby on the day but the *Journal* said, "the principal scene of the festivities being Wetheral Village Green." Afterwards a dinner was held at The Crown. At this part of the proceedings Mr Steel said, "a sufficient supply of water had always been one of the great drawbacks to the development of Wetheral."

WETHERAL, &c., WATER SUPPLY.

RULES AND REGULATION

FOR THE GUIDANCE OF

CONSUMERS OF WATER

AND THE

CONDITIONS

UNDER WHICH THE

Rural District Council of Carlisle

AGREE TO

SUPPLY THE SAME.

ENACTED 1895.

CARLISLE :
PRINTED BY STEEL BROTHERS, ENGLISH STREET.

Carlisle Library

Keith Simmonds (both images)

Above: Testing the water pressure at the switch on at Wetheral in 1895.

Above: Roadside well at Wetheral dedicated to St Cuthbert and restored in 1897 and 2001, the latter with money left over from the Millennium celebrations. Sources of water were always a problem when the river was the only alternative.

Left: Turning the water on at Hard Bank in 1895.

Coronations & Jubilees

Jean Ruddick

Michael Finlay

Above: Medals above were struck for the Wetheral celebration of the Coronation of King Edward VII. This event was originally scheduled for 26 June 1902, but Edward had to undergo an emergency appendectomy operation, so the Coronation was postponed until 9 August 1902.

Above: Bonfire at Corby Castle, 22 June 1911, in commemoration of the Coronation of King George V and Queen Mary.

Right: The Pageant held on Wetheral Village Green, 12 May 1937, to celebrate the Coronation of King George VI. Wetheral Cross can be seen in the background.

Below: Celebrations at Great Corby on 6 May 1935 for the Silver Jubilee of George V and Queen Mary. The banner says "God Bless their Majesties".

Keith Simmonds

Reg Elliot

Keith Simmonds

Above: Jubilee celebrations on the Green at Wetheral on 6 May 1935.

Wetheral School

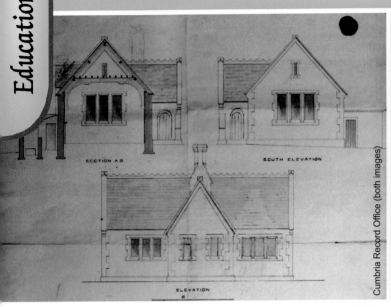

Cumbria Record Office (both images)

Above: Front and side elevations of the new school built in 1852 next to the Green.

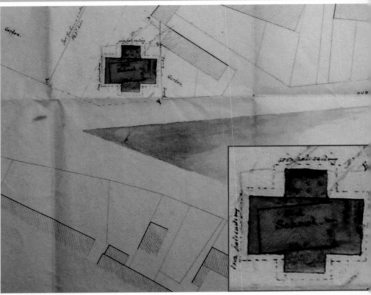

Above: Plan showing the proposed new 1852 school which was situated east of the Green.
Inset: On this enlargement from the above plan the new school can be seen superimposed on the old.

Mannix & Whellan's *History, Gazetteer and Directory of Cumberland*, 1847 records that, "In 1760, Thomas Graham left, for educating poor children of Wetheral quarter, £60, which by an accumulation of interest has increased to £65. This sum was expended in the purchase of a cottage and garden, now yielding about £4 a year, which, with about three roods of land, allotted upon an enclosure worth 10s. a year, is paid to a schoolmaster, who, on that account, instructs a few labourers' children of Wetheral." This is the first recorded school in the village and it was sited to the east of the Green.

In 1852 a new school, designed by James Stewart, was built on the site of the old one (see above right). and Thomas Forsyth was the first schoolmaster. He held this post until 1856 when he was appointed schoolmaster to the County Gaol, Carlisle. Mr Amos was the next schoolmaster of the National School (as it was then known) and he was succeeeded, on 8 January 1872, by James Livesey, who was to be in charge for the next 39 years until his retirement in 1911. In 1875 the school was replaced by another new building

on Cumwhinton Road at the southern entrance to the village and so James Livesey became the first master at this new site. According to the school records Miss Livesey was paid as a pupil teacher for four years and then she became assistant teacher.

On 1 September 1891 school fees from the children were abolished and a fee grant was paid to the school in lieu of the fees. James Livesey lived in the school house built to the north of the school until his retirement on 9 June 1911, after 39 years 5 months as master. Henry Caton then took over and, at the same time, Miss Arms moved to Wetheral as assistant teacher. Wetheral school continued to provide education for children in the village until 1977 when it finally closed. For much of this time it was an infants school

Keith Simmonds

Above: This photograph, circa 1874, with James Livesey, headmaster, was probably taken at the closure of the National School on the Green.

Above: Wetheral School class of 1957 with Mrs Carey, headteacher.
Back row left to right: Margaret Downie, Ann Patrick, David Stevens, John Fisher, Jennifer Robinson.
Front row left to right: Keith Meekley, unknown, unknown, Keith Simmonds, Julia Graham, Gabrielle Dalton, John Mc Ritchie (next to Mrs Carey), Kevin Macrory, unknown, Anthony Little, Richard Jennison.

and when children reached the age of seven they moved on to either Scotby or Great Corby School. Nowadays the building is still in use by local organisations such as Brownies, Rainbows, a creche, and a play group.

Keith Simmonds

Above: The new school on Cumwhinton Road opened in 1875, closed in 1977.

Above: James Livesey pictured outside the school house with members of his family at his retirement in June 1911. The school house is now used by a hairdressing business.

Bowling Club

Above: This photo shows how close the Edenside green was to Corby Bridge.

Left: A pre-war view, probably in 1912, showing a mixture of bowlers, those from the rifle club wilth their guns.

Joseph Farrer (see page 43) was the tenant at Edenside, a house that had a large garden in the former quarry beside Corby Bridge. In 1906, soon after the formation of the Wetheral and Corby Rifle and Bowling Club, the garden was sub-let by Mr Farrer to the club. This arrangement worked well because Farrer, a keen bowler and shooter himself, acted as the groundsman. A pavilion was built in 1912. Most of the younger members of the rifle club, a total of 25, joined the colours on the outbreak of war. A groundsman was appointed in 1917 and in 1919 the club was affiliated to the Border Counties Bowling Association. Formerly membership was restricted to residents of Wetheral but in1923 this rule was relaxed, bringing in much needed new members. However in 1924 Mr Farrer relinquished his tenancy of Edenside and this could have left the club homeless, but the new tenant, Mr Bulman, continued to sub-let to them.

In 1937 the rifle club closed down due to falling membership and, as the tenancy was not permanent and the location was not ideal, it was decided to look around for a more suitable site. Then a breakaway Linton Bowling Club was formed at Great Corby (see next page). The Wetheral Club played at Great Corby on a temporary basis until a lease was obtained (in June 1954) for their present ground. It took time to prepare the ground which was officially opened on 27 June 1959 and a bower followed soon after. Wetheral Bowling Club flourishes today in their replacement bower with modern facilities, opened on 3 June 1995.

"What led me to take up this game was that my father, J S Farrer, made the bowling green in his garden (at Wetheral, which was originally a croquet lawn) and I helped him, cutting it and rolling it each day so keeping it in good order for the players. I became the first lady member."

Mrs F M Irving writing in December 1961.

Below: The Wetheral Club in action at the Plains Road Green in July 2008.

Linton Club

In 2000 Gordon Finlinson, the then Hon Secretary of the Linton Bowling Club, Great Corby, wrote a brief history of the club. He stated that, "It seems to have been an ambition of Mr William Linton of Hill House, Great Corby and owner of Linton Tweeds, Carlisle, to provide recreational facilities for the residents of Great Corby." To this end he purchased, "a plot of land adjacent to Sandy Lane from a local farmer for the sum of £233.16s.0d, and four trustees were appointed with three in reserve ... The first priority was the construction of a bowling green and, although there was enough land to make a tennis court and a putting green, the latter two projects never materialised."

Gordon continued, "By 1937 the work was completed and Mr Linton became the first President of the club. He later became Life President and this arrangement has continued within the Linton family to the present time ... Linton B C has long been involved in friendly rivalry with Wetheral B C, it being recorded that a trophy in memory of Mr T J Thompson (a member of both clubs), was presented for a competition to be played annually between the male members of the two clubs and continues to the present day ... The Ladies of Linton and Wetheral have recently engaged in an annual competition for what is known as the *Doug Furlow Trophy* presented by Mrs Furlow of Wetheral Bowling Club in memory of her husband. ... During the 1950s the Ladies section of the club was particularly strong as, in 1958, the CWBA Rosalind Trophy was won by Madge Armstrong, Gladys Williams, Isobelle Sloan and Catherine Lawson, these ladies being County players."

In 1965 membership was recorded as 75 including social members and the facilities were seen to be inadequate and so a tea room was erected and opened on 1 October 1966. Further improvements followed, designed and supervised by Cyril Armstrong, a Past President of the club. The bower and tea room were connected and updated kitchen and toilet facilities were added, culminating in an extension to the bower in 2007. Apart from a small grant from Carlisle Council the improvements have been financed by donations and efforts of members. Like the Wetheral Club the Linton Bowling Club is a flourishing and active organisation to this day.

"In 1946 a minor crisis occurred in that the base of the flagpole was rotting and consequently six ft was removed at a cost of £2.10.0d, but this amount did include repainting.
The blackout curtains which disappeared during the early part of the war mysteriously reappeared in 1947."

Gordon Finlinson writing in 2000.

Right: The TJ Thompson trophy being fought out in inclement weather in July 2008 at the Linton Club.

Recreation Ground

Cumberland News

Above: The opening of the children's play area in 1991. Joe Armstrong is on the left, and John Amos, Mayor of Carlisle, is on the right.

Left: Workmen clearing up around the newly built children's play area.

Joe Armstrong

The recreation ground at Great Corby is part of Great Corby Castle Estate. In 1953 Colonel Levin, who occupied the castle at that time and was agent for Lady Lawson, was authorised to offer a lease on the field for £3 a year to the parish council.

The conversion of the field into the excellent recreation facility that it now is was achieved primarily by the hard work of Joe Armstrong (see page 31), who for many years was a Parish Councillor at Great Corby. For the next thirty years or so the field was used for village football, cricket, galas and general recreation, the facility being managed and looked after by Joe and his recreation ground committee. The one thing lacking was a proper play facility for the younger children in the village. Joe and his committee set about putting this right by raising money and applying for grants. The result was that in 1991 the new children's play area was opened by the Mayor of Carlisle, John Amos.

Since that time the new owner of the castle, Lord Balleyedmond, has agreed to extend the lease and a new Trustees and Management Committee for all of the facilities in the village, including the village hall, has been set up. Lord Balleyedmond very kindly donated £25,000 to the committee to help get them started. To date this has resulted in the re-furbishment of the village hall, the purchase of a new grass cutter and, at the time of writing, the changing rooms are being re-furbished.

Cumberland News

Joe Armstrong

Right: Youngsters from the village waiting for their turn on the swing!

Left: Trying out the new equipment at the opening of the play area.

Galas and Fetes

Left: Sky divers landing at the gala in 1990, a surprising attraction for such a small village.

Below: Children watching a Punch and Judy Show (would this be acceptable today?).

John Storr

The recreation ground is a great asset to the village. It is the home ground for the village football and cricket teams as well as providing the village youngsters with a safe area to play.

In addition it has been used for important events over the years such as Coronation and Jubilee celebrations and for occasional events such as summer fetes and gala days.

Right: The girls' sack race at the 1990 summer fete. The weather was obviously very hot.

Below: A very traditional event - dancing round the maypole in 1990.

Moore (both images)

Brooks (both images)

Right: Childrens' fancy dress in 1990, waiting for the judges.

The Forge at Great Corby is part of the Castle Estate. The arched building was erected in 1833 as a blacksmith's shop with a covered open space intended to represent Vulcan's Forge (in Greek mythology Vulcan is the god of fire and the blacksmith who forged weapons for many of the gods and heroes).

This was the smithy for the estate and the village. More recently it has been a car repair workshop.

In the late 1800s the village blacksmith was Tom Bowman. He retained that position for many years and can be seen on the postcard of the forge on page 31.

Ashley Kendall

Above: A postcard view of the village before the road was metalled.

Dorothy Carruthers

Left: The Bowman family outside their Great Corby home.

Right: Wetheral Smithy in the first quarter of the 20th century.
Tommy Marshal is on the right of the picture.

Below: The gate on Wetheral Cells.

David Park

Tommy Marshal was for many years the Blacksmith in Wetheral. The Smithy was at the south end of the village along the cemetery lonning. Later it was a small engineering workshop until it was finally demolished and replaced by two houses. Closer study of the two photographs shows the range of work done by the village blacksmith. Note the range oven waiting for repair in the picture below and the various agricultural implements, as well as the motorcycle in the picture above.

Cyril Middleham of Carlisle is Tommy's great nephew. When he was a youngster he recalls having a ride on Tommy's 'Fergie' tractor and trailer down to Wetheral Woods with a wrought iron gate for fixing to the entrance of Wetheral Cells (see page 7). The gate is still there over fifty years later.

Below: The smithy in the 1950s when an engineering workshop had been added. Soon after it was replaced by two houses (left).

Below: This photograph from 1912 shows a young Tommy Marshal and apprentice practising their craft at his smithy in Wetheral.

Evelyne Whitfield

Adams Family

Wetheral Village Hall

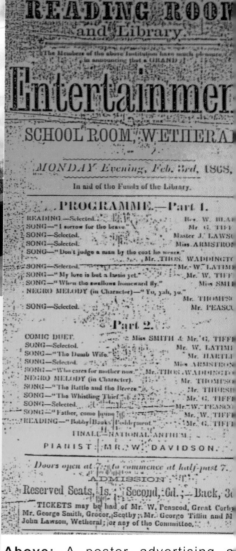

In 1991 to mark the centenary of the Village Hall a booklet was produced. It explained that the hall was, "formerly the Wetheral Reading Room and Library ... as early as the middle of the 1800s the Committee had rented the second storey of a small cottage, a little nearer to the centre of the village than the present Village Hall and along the same road. This room was said to be 'a very primitive place' adjoining the Green and approached by a flight of wooden steps ... Inhabitants of the village led by Mr James Steel of Eden Bank ... took a very strong view that a place like Wetheral should have a proper Reading Room. They 'raised an agitation' to provide funds for the building of such a Reading Room ... The generous gift of 100 guineas from Mr John Scott really started the financial ball rolling ... Even the site was donated - by Mr M Huthart of Portland Square, Carlisle ... The building was completed in 1891 at a total cost of £810 13s 8d."

Over the years the Reading Room has provided a venue for local organisations and village events. Financial problems in the 1940s and 50s meant that the Committee had difficulty maintaining the fabric of the hall and could only act effectively as a hall letting committee.

The passage of the Recreational Charities Act of 1958 recognised Village Halls as charitable institutions and so the Constitution was changed and the Reading Rooms became known as the Village Hall, allowing it access to much needed grants. The Hall is still well used by the village as is evidenced by the recent Photographic Exhibition mounted by Keith Simmonds, who has kindly provided several of the historical photographs used in this book.

Above: A poster advertising a grand Entertainment in aid of the funds for the library dated 3 February 1868.

Below: An exhibition of photographs of Wetheral and district arranged in the Village Hall in May 2008 by Keith Simmonds.

Gareth Melvin

Gareth races to title glory

By Amanda Little

Gareth Melvin was born in December 1980 and grew up in Great Corby attending Great Corby School and later William Howard at Brampton. It was here that his ability at distance running first became apparent. In 1994 at the age of 12 he qualified for the Inter Counties Cross Country Championships in the U13 (under 13) age group coming first. Then, later in the same year, he achieved a 'new championship best' in the U15 North of England Championships running at the bottom of the age group. He finished off the year with a 3rd place in the Scottish National Championships U15 group, again at the bottom of the age group and running against others up to two years older than himself. In one year he had come from an unknown runner to an inter-county champion.

Linda Armstrong, recognising his ability, offered to coach Gareth on Corby field and at St Aidans Sports Centre and it was Linda, according to Gareth, that gave him the interest and enthusiasm to train seriously for future competition. This soon paid off when he ran in the English Schools Athletics Association Junior Boys Cross Country and qualified to represent England at international level. This resulted in a win in Ireland in the Junior Boys Cross Country International at Dungarvon, Co Waterford. Later the same year he achieved wins in three England championships, achieving championship bests at 3000m and 1500m as well as a first in the Safeway International Cross Country U15. In 1996 Gareth had further inter county wins and in December 1997 he came 5th, running for the North of England team in Brussels. Gareth ran for the Great Britain team in 1998 at Lisbon, coming 12th and his running career culminated in December 1999 when he came first running for the England team in Brussels. That was Gareth's last run as a junior U20 and since then he has contined to run but on a less competitive basis. He still lives in Great Corby, is a member of the Border Harriers and a fireman by profession.

SCHOOLBOY athlete Gareth Melvin is the toast of Cumbrian athletics after winning his second Inter-Counties Cross-Country Championship.

The Border Harrier cruised to victory in the under-15's boy's race in a time of 14.08 minutes — over 20 seconds ahead of his nearest rival, Colin Bolt, of Berkshire.

The success at Luton's Wigmore Valley Park was added to his Inter-Counties under-13's title, which he won two years ago.

The 15-year-old, from Great Corby, near Carlisle, had been working towards the race with coach Linda Armstrong for the past six months and both are delighted their hard work has paid off.

"Gareth ran an excellent race and this is a very big achievement for him," said Linda.

"This is the race we've aimed for since the beginning of the cross-country season and now his prospects are good if he continues the way he is."

Gareth now has his sights set on defending his Under-15's Northern Championships title in Lincoln in a fortnight.

After that he will compete in the English Schools Cross-Country Championships in Weymouth in March.

Although he will be at the bottom of his age group, he hopes his current form will see him pull off his second big win of the year.

● For a full report on Border youngsters' performances at the weekend's Inter-Counties see Friday's Cumberland News.

Race ace Gareth Melvin with coach Linda Armstrong

Cumbrian Newspapers

Linda Armstrong

Gareth (far left) in an early race on the field. His friend Rachel Armstrong (right) is winning!

Left: Gareth running at Bedford in 1995 to win the 3000m U15 UK Championship.

Right: Gareth with the international five mile cross country winner's award at Brussels.

Below: Gareth winning at Brussels in December 1999.

Gareth Melvin all three images

Rory Delap

Right: Rory (at the back) was used to winning when playing for his primary school, St Bede's, in Carlisle.

John Delap

Rory Delap was born in Sutton Coldfield but grew up in Great Corby, attending St Bede's primary school in Carlisle where his father was headteacher. He played for his school teams and was soon noticed for his talent. In 1993, aged 16 years three hundred and six days, he became the youngest ever player to appear for Carlisle when he came on for 30 minutes as substitute against Scarborough. In 1995 he helped Carlisle win promotion to Division 2 and only one year later he played for the Irish under 21 team against Norway. In February 1998 Rory transferred to Derby for a fee of £500,000 and he also appeared for the Republic of Ireland 'B' level team against Northern Ireland. In March 1998 he played his first game for Ireland at full international level against the Czech Republic. Currently he has been capped 11 times playing for the Republic.

HEAD BOYS . . . first year YTS players , Tony Hopper (left) and Rory Delap. Picture - MIKE SCOTT.

Cumbrian Newspapers

Unfortunately on Boxing Day 1998 Rory sustained a serious knee injury when playing against Everton, but he was still able to sign up for a new contract with Derby for the 1999-2000 season. On 10 July 2001 Rory transferred to Southampton Saints for a record £4 million, double the previous highest fee paid by the Saints. He was to play for them in the Premier League for the next four years until they were relegated to Division 1 in May 2005. Then in, January 2006, he was transferred to Sunderland Black Cats and in October 2006 went on loan to Stoke City. Unfortunately in October 2006 on his home debut for Stoke he broke his leg in two places when challenging for the ball, whilst playing against Sunderland. Nevertheless Stoke signed him permanently, although he was unable to play for the rest of the season. Since then Rory has played a vital role in Stoke's first attempt to get promotion to the Premiership. At the time off writing he is still playing for Stoke City.

John Delap

Upper Right: Brunton Babes Rory Delap (right) and Tony Hopper as YTS trainees for Carlisle United.

Left: Rory in action for Carlisle.

Right: Rory playing for the Irish Republic.

John Delap

Then and now

M Ferguson

Above: Looking towards Scotby Road when the pace of life was slower.

Above: The same view today.

Ashley Kendall

Above: The village shop with Fantails on the left. The view today is much obscured by extra vegetation compared with the 1930s view on the right.

Jeff Ferguson

Left: This view, probably taken from the upper storey of Lime House looking across the Green, has changed a lot in the last 138 years. It can be dated before 1872 when Oak Bank (later Killoran, see page 25) was built on the site of the cottages in the picture.

Left: This comparison view was taken from the boundary wall of Lime House. Corby woods cannot be seen in the background because of the increased vegetation in the foreground and the lower elevation from which the image was taken.

Then and now

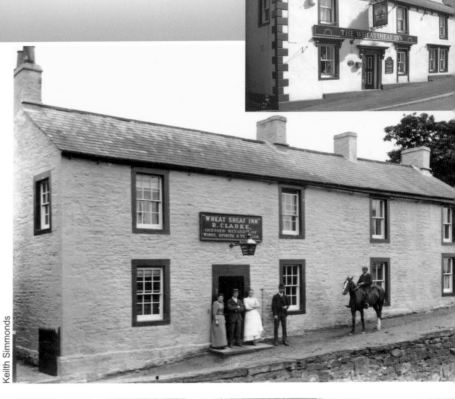

Right and above: The Wheat Sheaf Inn, open for much of the 19th century, is a rare survival when most pubs in Wetheral closed. This one came under State Control in 1916 until the 1973 sale. As can be seen it remains with little alteration, other than external decoration and an extra window, from this view of 1902.

Below right: A funeral cortege on its way from the church to the cemetery in the early 1900s.

Below: Little appears to have changed but a bungalow has appeared in the garden replacing the trees.
The railings have gone, the gate has become a vehicle access and there is unsightly street furniture.

Keith Simmonds

Reg Elliot

Below: Looking in the other direction at the turn of the 20th century.

Below: The view today shows extensions to the house on the right as well as the new bungalow on Richmond Hill.

Carlisle Library

Then and now

Above: Formerly two houses, one a farm, the Crown Inn flourished in the 19th century. When taken over by the Central Control Board in October 1916, which later became the State Management Scheme, an extra storey was added to the designs of Harry Redfern. Since privatisation in 1973 the hotel has been greatly extended to cater for 21st century needs.

Ashley Kendall

Left: The General Stores, still a shop today (above) was also a Post Office and Wetheral had its own postmark. Enterprising shopkeepers, over a number of years, produced and sold their own postcards of the village and surrounding area (see below).

Bottom right: The postcard shows Station Road and the Crown Hotel before 1910. On the modern photograph little appears to have changed apart from the increased foliage. However, a new road has been built to the left of the house (at the expense of the garden) leading to the new function room at the back of the hotel.

Then and now

Right: Church Brow, a winter view.
From the Green the road drops down to the ferry past the church and Fish Inn, seen at the bottom; which in this view is still in business. The right fork leads to Abbey Farm.

Below right: This more recent view, taken in summer, shows that the only change, apart from the vegetation, is the lack of the wooden fence.

Ashley Kendall

The former Fish Inn.

From the early 19th century newspaper reports give the names of licencees, activities there and the problems of drunkenness.

At the licensing sessions in February 1906 the decision was taken to close because of "ill conduct, drunkenness and bad situation concealed by the churchyard."

Guy Pawle

On 14 May 1907, the *Journal* reported on the sale of the "dwelling house recently occupied by Carlisle Old Brewery as tenants."
The auctioneer remarked, "that its position was second to none for doing a good summer business as a tea house." However, only six people attended the sale and five were bidders, Mr Reid securing the property for £325, changing the name to Ferry Hill House.

Inset: During restoration in the 1970s some of the painted advertising on the former pub was uncovered.

Left: Church Brow, Wetheral showing the Fish Inn when it was still a public house.

Oher.

Right: The view today of what is now Ferry Hill House and little has changed.

Anderson Robert: See page 26.

Anderson Thomas: See page 46.

Boag Alfred: Road carriage manufacturer who took over from Barton & Co at the Crescent in Carlisle. He is listed at Wood Grange, Wetheral in 1901 but emigrated to South Africa soon afterwards.

Bough Sam: 1822 - 1878 see pages 38 & 39.

Bowman Rev Edward Lawson: Born in Northamptonshire but had Cumbrian connections. Became a chaplain in the Royal Navy and and kept a diary of his experiences in the Crimea and the Indian Mutiny. Later postings were to North Africa and North America. Served as vicar of Alston until retirement at Wetheral with his two sisters. He died in 1890.

Crosthwaite Mrs: See page 27.

De Quincey Richard & Thomas: see pages 36 & 37.

Dunne Sir John: See page 26.

Elliot George: See page 23.

Farrer J S: 1860-1952 see page 43.

Howard Henry: 1757-1842 see pages 8,12,36 & passim.

Ismay John: Was a local business man operating from his Wetheral home as a seedsman and gun maker active in the late 1870s into the 1890s.

Kirkpatrick Margaret: 1900 - 1966, daughter of Thomas Lawson of Wetheral. A leading light in the WI, she wrote a history of the village which was published by Wetheral WI.

Kirtlan Lilian: The wife of a railwayman living at Wetheral in 1925 when she claimed to be a direct descendant of Sir John Jermy, Governor of Sierra Leone in 1840-41. A fortune of £7 - £10 million was waiting to be claimed.

Ling Christopher: See page 48.

Loftie Rev Arthur Gershom: 1843-1922. Born in Nice, son of J H Loftie of Tandragee, Co Armagh, was curate of Arthuret 1867-71, vicar of St Bridget, Beckermet 1871-94, rector of Great Salkeld 1894-1904 and rector of Wetheral 1904-1916, canon of Carlisle 1908-1922. In 1874 he married the youngest daughter of James Robert Grant of the Hill. but died without children. Was the author of a book on Wetheral.

Milburn John: A native of Great Corby he died in Egypt in 1905, the manager of the Cairo Locomotive Works.

Pedley Major J Cross: Resident of Wetheral and Scoutmaster. While serving in the army in World War 2 was taken prisoner by the Japanese being held at a notorious camp at Shirakawe on Formosa. Was awarded the Silver Wolf by the Chief Scout for his magnificent example while a POW.

Prescott Archdeacon JE: See page 19.

Rayson George: Lemonade and soda water manufacturer at Botchergate, Carlisle. His widow died in 1881 aged 77 at their house on Wetheral Plains.

Scott John: See page 25.

Bibliography

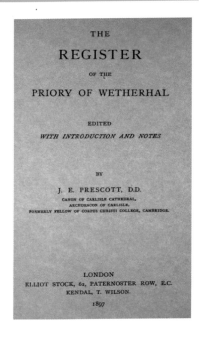

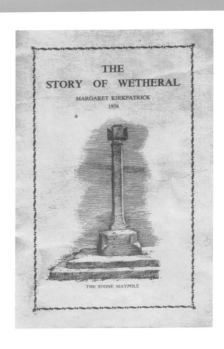

Margaret Kirkpatrick,
The Story of Wetheral, 1956.
re-published 1966 and 1969.

J E Prescott,
*The Register of the Priory
of Wetheral*, 1897.

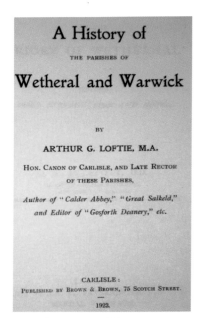

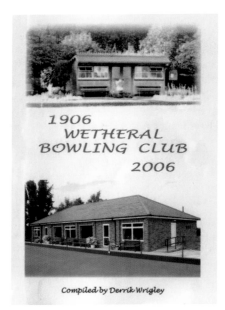

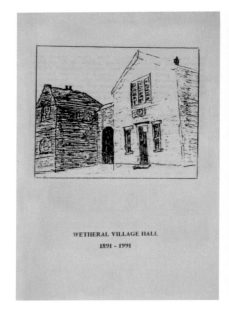

Arthur G Loftie
*A History of Wetheral
and Warwick*, 1923

Derrick Wrigley, compiler,
*Wetheral Bowling Club,
1906-2006.*

Compiler not named,
*Wetheral Village Hall,
1891-1991.*

Other sources consulted:- *The Citizen, Carlisle Journal (Journal), Carlisle Patriot, Carlisle Express, Cumberland Pacquet, Cumberland News,* William Hutchinson *History of Cumberland* 1794, J Scott Duckers *Handed Over,* Thomas De Quincey *The Stranger's Grave, History of NER Architecture, The Building News, Tinsley's Magazine, Times Literary Supplement,* Grevel Lindop *The Opium Eater, Daily Mail,* local directories, *The Architect, Handbook of the N&C Railway* 1851, Thurnam *Guide to Carlisle* 1821, Dorothy Wordsworth *Tour of Scotland, Transactions of Cumberland & Westmorland Antiquarian and Archaelogical Society,* Bailey and Cramp *Corpus of Anglo-Saxon Stone Sculpture, Place Names of Cumberland.*